FROM ADMIRAL TO CABIN BOY

by

ADMIRAL SIR BARRY DOMVILE
K.B.E., C.B., C.M.G.

The Boswell Publishing Co., Ltd.,
10, Essex Street, London, W.C.2.
1947

Reprint Edition, 2025
Dauphin Publications
www.Daupub.com

From Admiral to Cabin Boy

"No man will be a sailor who has contrivance enough to get himself into a jail; for being in a ship is being in a jail with the chance of being drowned . . . a man in jail has more room, better food, and commonly better company."

> Dr. Samuel Johnson.
> A.D. 1759.

TO

ALL MY FORMER SHIPMATES

ON BOARD

HIS MAJESTY'S STONE FRIGATE

ON

BRIXTON HILL

1940-1943

CONTENTS

	Page
FOREWORD	4
PREFACE	6
PROLOGUE (I to IV)	7-14
SCENARIO (I to LXXXI)	14-139
EPILOGUE (I to XXI)	139-163

AUTHOR'S NOTE.

This book was finished in 1943, but publication was delayed for several reasons, some obvious.   B.D.

FOREWORD

Barry Edward Domvile, son of the late Admiral Sir Compton Edward Domvile, G.C.B., G.C.V.O., started a brilliant career brilliantly. Born in 1878, in 1892 he passed first into H.M.S. Britannia, and, two years later emerged in the same coveted position. From 1894 to 1897 he served as a Midshipman under sail and steam. Sub-Lieutenant in 1898, he became, by special promotion, Lieutenant in the same year. Lieutenant and Gunnery-Lieutenant from 1898 to 1909, in 1906 he was awarded the Gold Medal of the Royal United Service Institution.

During 1910 and 1911, Domvile was in command of destroyers, and, when the first World War loomed on the horizon, was appointed Assistant Secretary to the Committee of Imperial Defence during war preparation. Throughout hostilities he commanded successively "Miranda," "Tipperary," "Lightfoot," "Arethusa," "Carysfort," "Centaur" and "Curacao"—destroyers, flotilla leaders and cruisers of the Harwich Force. For the three years preceding 1919, he served as Flag Captain to Admiral Sir Reginald Tyrwhitt.

For the following three years he was employed as Assistant Director and Director of the Plans (Policy) Division of the Admiralty Naval Staff, attending a number of conferences, including those at Paris, Brussels, Spa and San Remo, winding up with the Washington Naval Conference. From 1922 to 1925, he was Chief of Staff to Admiral Sir Osmond Brock, of the Mediterranean Fleet, and during 1925 and 1926 commanded the "Royal Sovereign," which has now been handed to the Soviet Union.

In 1927 he was promoted Rear-Admiral and up to 1930 held the important position of Director of Naval Intelligence. During 1930 and 1931, first as Rear-Admiral and then as Vice-Admiral, he commanded the Third Cruiser Squadron, Mediterranean Fleet. From 1932 to 1934 he was President of the Royal Naval College, Greenwich, and Vice-Admiral Commanding the War College. In 1936 he retired with the rank of Admiral.

In 1917, Captain Domvile was created a Companion of the Most Distinguished Order of St. Michael and St. George, and in 1922, as Commodore, a Companion of the Most Honourable Order of the Bath. Finally, in 1934, His Majesty King George V was pleased to honour him further by creating him a Knight Commander of the Most Excellent Order of the British Empire.

This was the record our misguided rulers saw fit to impugn. In 1940 the Home Secretary, Sir John Anderson, vainly attempted to abort this magnificent career by appointing the Admiral cabin boy at Brixton Prison: Anderson was succeeded shortly afterwards by Morrison, who at one time could be classed as a conscientious objector, and was author of an article taunting British soldiers and urging them not to fight for their country, but the Admiral held his position for three years, acquitting himself in his customary exemplary manner, save for a little lapse which took the form of manufacturing a stove, contrary to regulations, of an old tobacco tin, a lump of margarine and a piece of string.

Nothing could excuse delaying the reader from embarking upon this exciting and extraordinary story. He will find himself buffeted exhilaratingly upon the high seas of every human emotion before he reaches the port of his own judgment. Sir Barry Domvile is fortunate in one sense: he will not have to wait, as so many men who have suffered injustice have had to do, for the verdict of history to complete his vindication. Each successive year, like the one that has just passed, will provide fresh proof of his wisdom and foresight. Yet, since this must inevitably bring suffering to his fellow-countrymen, the Admiral, in his patriotism and the greatness of his heart, will be the first to deplore the fact.

In appraising him, the words of Horace rise readily to the mind: "The just man, firm to his purpose, is not to be shaken from his fixed resolve by the fury of a mob laying upon him their impious behests, nor by the frown of a threatening tyrant, nor by the dangers of the restless Adriatic, when the stormy winds do blow, nor by the loud peals of thunder as they rend the sky; even if the universe were to fall in pieces around, the ruins would strike him undismayed."

CUTHBERT REAVELY.

PREFACE

Many worthy individuals in their declining years yield to the temptation to inflict upon their fellow mortals accounts of their successful voyages through life in the various states to which it has pleased the Almighty to call them.

But whether we are in this way invited to read about a peasant becoming a peer, a waster achieving the Woolsack, or a congenital idiot attaining Cabinet rank, all these tales have one thing in common—they portray the hero on the upward grade, or in modern slang, on the 'up and up.'

Probably there will be a few minor setbacks during the Odyssey, which will only serve to enhance the subsequent ascents, culminating in the complete self-vindication, and presumably in the self-satisfaction, of the author.

But this tale, which I am offering to you at whatever price my publishers decide, is of a totally different order.

Alas, there is no sign of an ascent. The peak has been reached already before this dénouement begins. Only the downward slope is in view, and the pitch is so steep that it amounts almost to a fall, against which my family motto "Qui stat caveat ne cadat" warned me.

For this is the plain unvarnished tale of a retired admiral, living a happy, contented life and wanting nothing more, who, to his own amazement, became a cabin boy in one fell swoop.

I hasten to add that the cabin was in a prison, and that the prison was on Brixton Hill.

Some ill-natured people would call this cabin a cell, but if it is all the same to you, cabin sounds nicer, and gives this book a better title. So there you are.

If you are too tender-hearted to study such a calamity, stop right here. If, on the other hand, you feel that perchance there might be a lesson to be learnt from this horrid catastrophe, go right ahead.

But you must deduce the moral for yourself.

B.D.

ROBIN'S TREE,
ROEHAMPTON VALE,
LONDON, S.W.15.

PROLOGUE

I.

One of the crowning mercies vouchsafed to us mortals is our inability to gaze into the future; to know what is in store for us. Many people do not appear to appreciate this particular benefit, and endeavour by means of cards, tea-leaves, crystal-gazing, or other ju-ju, to force the Fates to show their hands. Poor deluded beings. They should count their blessings and leave well alone.

I only hope that the numerous fortune-tellers and necromancers in the world will not take these remarks in bad part, or think that I am trying to deprive them of their means of livelihood. Nothing is further from my intentions, which are stimulated mainly by the desire that others should profit by my experience. If my wife and I had been told when I retired from the Navy that, in less than four years' time we should be occupying cells in separate prisons, I cannot even imagine the dreadful anticipation that would have harassed us during the period of suspense, and which we were spared by the beneficent dispensations of the Almighty.

We should have indulged in exhaustive studies of the penal code in a fruitless endeavour to discover the particular crime for which this penalty would be exacted. What on earth could it be?

No forms of fraud or violence have ever been hobbies of ours. Of course one of us might have had the misfortune to iron out some luckless pedestrian under the onslaught of the family juggernaut, and this knowledge would have led undoubtedly to nervousness at the wheel. But it was unlikely that both of us would suffer such a calamity. Our minds would have run the gamut of every sort of ill-luck and we should have spent a miserable instead of a very happy life.

All the guesswork under the sun would never have brought us anywhere near the truth. And yet when the blow fell and the prison gates closed behind us, the experience was not nearly so bad as our imaginations would have painted it in anticipation. Personally I was able to preserve a feeling of complete detachment to events which many people of different temperament might have found very hard to bear. I felt as if I was someone else watching my own adventures with interested concern—nay, if I must admit it, almost with amusement. I never had any sense of bitterness. I realised that we were living in queer times, and that people must be expected to act in a most unusual manner. I was certainly not disappointed in this.

I had no apprehension in regard to what my friends might be thinking of me, because I knew that all those who were worth calling friends would never imagine for one moment that I had done anything that could be classed as improper: on the contrary. And the others? Well, they just didn't matter. Indeed it is an irony of fate that the better the motives for one's actions, the more likely they are to be misjudged by the ignorant and ill-informed.

II.

The cause of our downfall was our efforts to improve the friendly relations and mutual understanding between the British and German nations before the war put a stop to all such activities.

The misfortunes suffered by ourselves and our allies in the spring and early summer of 1940 sealed our fate.

The successes attending German arms in their inroads into their neighbours' lands, were accompanied in each case by considerable assistance from within the invaded countries.

It was only to be expected, therefore, that the threat of invasion to our own sacred shores would produce an agitation in the National Press in regard to similar possibilities within our own boundaries. All those who had worked for a friendly understanding with Germany as preferable to the catastrophe of a world war, were at once under suspicion, however well-meant their intentions. Hardly flattering, but easily understood, especially by those of us who have studied the sources of inspiration of our national daily papers.

The country was in a state of panic following the evacuation of the British Army from the Continent, and all sorts of absurd rumours were in circulation.

The first round-up of political suspects took place at the end of May. We spent the month of June in Dorset where our host was endeavouring patriotically to reclaim some poor lands for the plough. The countryside insisted that he was making a landing-ground for German parachute troops. It would have been easy to laugh at such absurdities, if they had not been so serious from our point of view. Suspicion was rife. Our host became the target for the wildest rumours, and one fine day we were left without him. He was on his way to Brixton Prison.

At Petty Sessions and Assizes savage sentences were being passed for the most trivial misdemeanours, which a few months earlier would have landed both magistrates and judges in the pillory of public opinion. Now they were patriotic heroes.

When two Jewish gentlemen in the House of Commons made enquiries in regard to my political health, and asked why my son and I were not shut up, I felt that the moment was near. We had not long to wait.

III.

On Sunday, July 7th, at about 9 p.m., a few days after our return to our home in Roehampton, a little party arrived from Scotland Yard armed with a search warrant. The only one I can identify, besides Inspector Keeble, was a Jew called Abrahams who accompanied the police, and boasted subsequently of his achievement to his friends, from one of whom it reached me.

The Inspector went through my pockets whilst my wife went upstairs with the female of the cop species. A thorough search of the whole house was then made, special attention being paid to hidden arrangements for wireless and telephonic communication. Both these coverts having been drawn blank, the posse were content with impounding a number of innocuous books and documents. No, content is the wrong word, for they returned on more than one occasion subsequently, after we had retired from public life, and at one of these visits they removed a valuable pair of 12-bore guns, for which a receipt was refused.

Owing to the laws of Meum and Tuum, as between subject and State, having been recently abrogated as a Defence Measure, they were strictly within their rights, although I must admit that when I heard of it I was much annoyed at the thought of some zealous Home Guard enjoying the use of my weapons against some inoffensive motorist who might fail to hear his orders to 'Stand and Deliver' at a barricade. I never imagined for one moment that they would be required for any more worthy purpose.

The most suspicious article removed was a clue to a treasure hunt which I conducted in Malta in 1931. Here it is:—

> Go to Ma to ask her where
> Is the hidden Bare Paw's lair?
> Has he really lost a ball?
> Is it gone beyond recall?
> Mother says it's easy—see
> Just as simple as BC
> Mother, I must ask you pray
> Wherefore do you ban an A?

The answer to this nonsense consisted of two pieces of jewellery hidden in a banana and a tomato, and must have caused Scotland Yard many an anxious moment. The members of the Bare Paws Club will read this item with delight—the biter bit. The origin of this club is lost in antiquity, but it had something to do with the shortage of kid gloves just after the last war, which made it imperative that the nightly hospitality of Malta should be sampled gloveless. I think we were defying some Palace Edict of dear old Lord Plumer's, but I cannot remember exactly.

To return to our muttons, or rather our cops, when the search was over for the night, Inspector Keeble suddenly confronted my wife and me with warrants for our detention under the famous 18B Regulation.

This came as a shock to us all, as we had got the impression that the search had completed our trials for the day. However, there was nothing to be done. My wife packed a bag for each of us, the Inspector and the lady-cop supplying advice as to the latest prison fashions. I was relieved to hear that the Broad Arrow had passed out of favour, as I had always thought it so conspicuous and unbecoming.

Then we bade a sad farewell to our happy little household of children, servants and dogs, and were driven away to an unknown destination. This turned out to be a London police station, where, at one o'clock in the morning we were deposited, and locked into cells on opposite sides of the corridor.

I only hoped that this would not be my home for long, as I had never been partial to a water-closet in my bedroom, especially one of such doubtful antecedents as the specimen upon which I found myself gazing with dislike.

The bed was hard—bare boards usually are—but I was soon to get used to such a trifling inconvenience. I was alone, and that was to the good, and I managed to get a certain amount of repose after the excitements of the night.

The next morning brought a palatable breakfast, and a little later the Inspector returned to claim our bodies. Henceforward I was to be just a 'b o d y' for quite a long time.

My wife and I were allowed to say goodbye to one another—God bless the bravest woman I have ever known—and then she was driven off to another unknown destination, whilst I had to await the Inspector's return.

When I got outside my doss-house ultimately, lo and behold, there was St. Michael's, Chester Square, where our daughter had been christened when we lived in Elizabeth Street just after the last war. So we had spent the night in Gerald Road police-station, the home of rest to which many a drunk who had found the wines and spirits of Pimgravia too strong for his balance, had been conveyed by a friendly policeman in the good old days when we lived round the corner. I was surrounded by friendly memories; so near and yet so far.

Just around another corner, in Eaton Place, the American naval attaché, Billy Galbraith, a dear friend of ours, had played a fine practical joke on his guests at a dance, with the assistance of this same B Division from Gerald Road Police-station.

A posse had turned up in the ballroom by special arrangement, whilst our hostess shouted at the top of her voice, "Boys, the house is pinched." Many were completely taken in. I was so certain that they were not real rozzers, that I danced with one of them, and never heard the end of it from Billy, who always prefaced his visits to me at the Admiralty by saying "Have you been dancing with any policemen lately?" How we all laughed when the jest was revealed, after we had recovered from the shock.

And now I *was* pinched in deadly earnest; but this was no time for meditation, however agreeable. Forward into the waiting car with the Inspector, and on across the river to the Alma Mater of male 18B's, Brixton Prison, my home on the hill for many a long day to come.

But before reaching those forbidding gates in Jebb Avenue, and describing my experiences as a guest of the Government, the time has come to call a temporary halt to this Pilgrim's Progress, and to consider at some length the background of events leading to this climax.

IV.

Patriotism is a much abused word in the English language. The patriot of my youth is the traitor of today, if he limits his love to his own country. He is expected to extend it to all other "peace-loving" countries to a similar degree. The term has become a misnomer, and a lot of confusion is caused.

Dr. Johnson has defined patriotism as the last refuge of the scoundrel. Whilst not prepared to go so far as the learned wit in thus describing the members of a British Government, it must be admitted that they do place great reliance on the term 'patriotism' to cover up their misdeeds in time of stress. That valuable soporific "My country right or wrong" has provided a balm for many uneasy consciences and timid natures. It can be obtained free of charge at any Government Office. I find myself unable to indulge in this type of 'pipe-smoking.' Whilst fully prepared at all times to perform any service to which I may be called, in support of "my country right or wrong," I am not going to call a thing right, when I am convinced it is wrong: that would not be patriotism at all, but merely opportunism or cowardice.

So firmly was I convinced on this occasion that the course upon which the ship of state was being navigated by its bemused pilots was unnecessarily hazardous, that I tried to do what little is possible to any individual to open the eyes of my fellow-countrymen to the dangers ahead. Win, lose, or draw, I could see nothing but disadvantage to our Empire in the contemplated crusade on behalf of what passes for democracy: in all three cases there would be a *'tertius gaudens,'* who did not answer to the name of Britain.

I did not approach the subject from a political point of view: I am no politician, and have never belonged to any political party, where one is liable to develop an enthusiasm for some particular creed, which blinds one to the larger national and imperial issues. On this occasion our politicians were so badly bitten by the international bug, that the frenzy thus engendered appeared to have eclipsed the real interests of their own land, which must be the first consideration of any government finding itself in temporary command of the national fortunes.

As I saw the matter, we were making the most determined and unnecessary attempt at national suicide ever recorded in history. I was regarding the situation from the strategical aspect, about which I have some knowledge, which helps me to judge whether our foreign policy is being developed on sound lines.

Policy and Strategy should be like Siamese twins, inseparable in conception and conduct.

For various reasons, which we shall examine, this principle had been entirely neglected since the Great War, with the result that we found ourselves in a very disadvantageous strategic situation in the event of another war.

So neglecting Benjamin Franklin's advice that little boats should keep near shore, I launched my frail barque on the high seas of controversy, and although the storms and perils which I was called upon to face ended eventually in shipwreck on Brixton Hill, I have no regrets whatever for undertaking the voyage, as I should always have reproached myself if I had failed to do my utmost to draw attention to the contemplated betrayal of all true British interests. It is a matter for deep regret, however, that my misgivings have been only too completely justified by the passage of events.

SCENARIO

I.

I have had exceptional opportunities during my career as a naval officer, of observing the conduct of high policy in Empire affairs. Before the Great War I was blooded in these matters by a two years apprenticeship to Sir Maurice Hankey, now Lord Hankey, as one of the assistant secretaries to the Committee of Imperial Defence. I saw the politicians both at work and play, and obtained a valuable experience in the working of the Government machine.

I enjoyed myself enormously, and had a great admiration for the way in which Mr. Asquith, later Lord Oxford, handled his team, who were not always easy. One of the most difficult was Winston Churchill, at that time First Lord of the Admiralty, and destined at a later date to play heavy lead in the Westminster Marionette Theatre during the most critical moments in the history of the British Empire.

From that time onwards I had a strong suspicion that there was some mysterious Power at work behind the scenes controlling the actions of the figures visibly taking part in the Government of the country. I had not the least idea whence this power emanated, nor could I gauge the strength of its influence. I was in far too humble a position to make such lofty discoveries. Still the feeling persisted. We always vaguely referred to this hidden control amongst ourselves as the Treasury.

I am convinced now that one elderly peer in particular took a prominent part in this secret direction.

On the surface he was merely a political busybody, who wove his spells in an unobtrusive manner. As far as I can remember he held no government office, but flitted round like a bat in the sunlight, and appeared to have the entrée to all the sacred chambers of the inner political world. Perhaps I may still discover some day what his game was. He was a constant visitor to our offices in Whitehall Gardens, and a source of irritation to Hankey, upon whose valuable time he made considerable inroads.

Hankey had succeeded Sir George Clarke, later Lord Sydenham, who had not proved sufficiently adaptable as a Secretary, because he was too fond of devising his own policy. When he was translated elsewhere, Hankey, who had been one of his assistant secretaries and originally a captain in the Royal Marines, was elevated to this important post, at a very youthful age, and held it for many years, with great distinction. Hardworking and very capable, he, too, managed to get a good bit of his own way, but in a more tactful manner than his predecessor.

This mysterious Power, to which I have been referring, will be constantly appearing in the course of this narrative. A short distinctive title will be a convenience. Let us christen it Judmas, because, as I discovered at a much later date, its source is the Judaeo-Masonic combination, which has wielded such a baneful influence in world history for many centuries.

II.

After watching the Liberal Government embark reluctantly on the war, I went off to sea for the duration: when it was all over, I joined the Naval Staff at the Admiralty as Assistant-director, and later on, Director of Plans.

In this post I found myself in constant attendance at the interminable international conferences which were held during the next three years.

Amongst others, Spa, Paris, Brussels, San Remo, and Washington; all found me picking up the crumbs that fell from the political tables. In this way I gained considerable experience of the big political figures of the day from the various countries, and their devious ways, which were rather hard of comprehension to one brought up in the more straightforward methods of a disciplined service.

From that time onwards, I watched with apprehension the gradual departure of our foreign policy from the sound strategical principles upon which it should be based, and which it was my duty to study.

III.

Sea Power has always been the basis of our system of Empire Defence. This Empire consists of widely-scattered territories situated in all the oceans, so that it was truly said, originally, I think, by John Wilson, that the sun never sets upon them. Envious and unkind foreigners say that this is because the Almighty cannot trust us in the dark.

However that may be, the men who built this Empire, and who were a great deal wiser than those who are doing their best to lose it today, arranged their conquests and acquisitions so that any enemy contemplating attack would be compelled to transport his forces overseas.

There are a few exceptions: Canada has a long common frontier with the United States, which it is their mutual boast needs no guard: India has a long and difficult northern frontier: but in the main, attack can only come by sea.

Therefore, if we control the seas, no danger need be anticipated, and it is on this principle that the Empire and its chain of communications were built up.

The advent of air power has modified this immunity to a certain extent, and has made naval defence a more difficult problem, but it is still true to say today that sea power remains the basis of our defence system.

IV.

In home waters, the proximity of the heart of the Empire to foreign territories has involved extra precautions. For many years British foreign policy vis-a-vis Europe has been based on three major principles:—

1. Reluctance to see the Low Countries, Holland and Belgium, pass under the control of any Great Power.
2. Unwillingness to see any Great Power attain a dominant position in Europe.

This principle, known as the balance of power, aimed at dividing Europe into two main camps of more or less equal strength, as a deterrent to the temptation of attacking one another; an immoral but moderately effective policy. Great Britain, sitting on Europe's doorstep, endeavoured to pull the strings accordingly, and was thus deeply involved in European politics.

3. Extreme reluctance to see any European Power, or, for the matter of that, any other Power at all, build a powerful navy as an obvious threat to British sea communications; natural, but difficult to justify in perpetuity.

Kaiser Wilhelm's attempt to violate this principle led Britain to align herself with France and Russia at the commencement of this century. Insistence on German Sea Power at that time was a short-sighted policy on the Kaiser's part. He should have waited until he was more firmly established in his European aims, before antagonising unnecessarily the rulers of the British Empire, who have always been very touchy, and rightly so, from their point of view, over this naval business.

The German seaboard is situated at a great strategic disadvantage relatively to the British Isles, which straddle its connections with the outer seas. This handicap could only have been surmounted by vast naval predominance on the part of Germany, and to this the Kaiser never aspired. The policy he attempted would only have enabled him to annoy, and not to dictate. Internationally this was a mistake, as are all half-hearted measures.

V.

At the end of the Great War, which we know now was only the first round in a much more world-wide contest, existing conditions made the establishment of a durable peace very difficult. Large-scale wars had been so completely out of fashion for a long time, that the ingredients essential to the successful negotiation of a Peace Treaty had been forgotten.

Of course there were the history books, but how could these be expected to weigh against the confident anticipations of modern democracies whose arms had been victorious, and whose lust for vengeance had been fanned by the Press and by their raucous politicians to such a white heat, that they would never have been content with any milk-and-water peace conditions?

It is impossible to be nourished on a diet of 'Hang the Kaiser' and 'Squeeze Germany until the pips squeak,' and then to be satisfied with good plain peace food, easy of digestion.

So the various peace treaties were dictated by victors who naturally took the lion's share of the spoils. Naturally also, the largest lions took the biggest shares, which led to dissatisfaction in the den itself, as happened in the case of Italy.

It has been the fashion, especially in recent years, to lay the blame for all the world's troubles on the Treaty of Versailles and its smaller brethren, on the grounds of their unfairness to the vanquished. This philanthropic ideal is a false criterion. Nations that have embarked on the ordeal of battle, must expect to pay if they lose. *Vae Victis.* Their whining leaves me cold.

The merit of a treaty of peace does not lie so much in the actual test of the conditions to be observed, as in the wisdom and foresight exercised in respect to the durable nature of the treaty. To some this may appear a distinction without a difference, but it is not so. For example, if the peace conditions are harsh, it is obviously necessary to arrange that they can be enforced and maintained without danger of retaliation, involving a further breach of the peace.

To make a peace treaty which can neither be expected to endure, nor yet to be capable of enforcement, even after a further recourse to arms, is just silly.

It is from this point of view that the Treaty of Versailles and its satellites must be condemned. Old Clemenceau boasted that the French were carrying the war on into the peace, but he does not appear to have given much thought to the effort necessary to maintain this delectable state of affairs.   Perhaps he was too old.

This is no question of being wise after the event. Many eminent men of knowledge and understanding raised their voices and flourished their pens, in protest against some of the more blatant follies in the Peace Treaties, notably those in connection with the Polish settlement, which were likely to lead to further warfare. Unfortunately many of these same voices and pens were just as fluent subsequently when raised in outcry against Germany and other countries, which had been on the losing side during the Great War, and had found themselves at a later date strong enough to try and set aright what they considered to be wrong.

VI.

A novel and incalculable turn was given to the strategic conditions of the world by the terms of the Peace Treaties, or rather by the Covenant of the League of Nations, which was incorporated in the Treaties.

By this instrument an endeavour was made to impose a system of collective security upon the members of the League against any nation deemed guilty of aggression. This collective security was intended to replace the old balance of power in Europe.

By agreeing to its provisions the British Empire signed a blank cheque as far as strategical commitments were concerned.

There are several claimants to the authorship of the League, of which President Wilson was the most ardent sponsor. In reality the idea emanated from Judmas, as was revealed at a later date.

Had I known then what I do now, I should have been more suspicious of its *bona fides.* The motives announced were impeccable. Nobody could find fault with the idea of providing international collaboration in social and economic problems, of preserving harmony amongst the members, and of punishing the offenders in the event of discord. It was an admirable notion to establish a forum to which all nations could bring their wants and grievances.

A little judicious money-lending on the 'side' was included, as no one can be expected to indulge in high principles without the concomitant 'interest.' So the three golden balls were hoisted at Geneva over the slogan "The Old Firm, Usury As Usual."

VII.

The League accomplished much valuable work in dealing with social and economic matters, but broke down utterly on the question of Collective Security, and the contributions in armed forces thereby demanded from the various members.

The system was never given a fair chance, as the United States refused to accept responsibility for their President's baby, and remained outside the League. This was a crushing blow. It is an ironical thought in regard to Collective Security, that of our two principal allies today, the United States and Russia, the former never joined the League, and the latter was expelled for breaking the rules.

Another fatal handicap to the success of the League was the inclusion of the Covenant of the League in the text of the Peace Treaties, whose integrity the League was intended to maintain, in spite of some pious provisions for their rectification contained in the Covenant.

It was not surprising that the 'Have-not' countries, as they soon came to be called, viewed the League with suspicion, entered it reluctantly when permitted to do so, and subsequently withdrew when they found that their claims were coldly received.

With the breakdown in the system of Collective Security, due to the difficulty in obtaining agreement on coercive measures, the League fell gradually into discredit as the years slipped by, and the nations of the world drifted hopelessly towards the next struggle. It was a tragedy that no great statesman arose anywhere with sufficient influence and foresight to arrest this drift, and to propound the policies essential to an avoidance of further conflict. A fatalistic paralysis appeared to have smitten all the Governments, but Judmas was busily at work behind the scenes.

VIII.

Apart from the general uncertainty of strategic commitments arising out of the League, one definitely risky undertaking was assumed by Great Britain, in accepting the mandate for Palestine. It had been hoped that the United States would have shouldered this burden, and thus definitely shown a desire to partake in world-wide responsibilities.

But the American Government's refusal to join the League put this out of court, and the British were morally bound to act as substitute, in view of the famous declaration made by Mr. Arthur Balfour, later Lord Balfour, when Foreign Secretary in November, 1917. This runs:—
"His Majesty's Government view with favour the establishment in Palestine of a national home for the Jewish people, and will use their best endeavours to facilitate the achievement of that object, it being understood that nothing shall be done which may prejudice the civil and religious rights of existing non-Jewish communities in Palestine, or the rights and political status enjoyed by the Jews in any other country."

By assuming this fresh responsibility, the British Government made a dangerous departure from the sound principles of defence which had regulated their policy hitherto.

Palestine lies in the hub of the Great Continent formed by Europe, Asia, and Africa, and is readily accessible to attack from the landward side.

Any defence forces required in time of crisis must be brought across the seas, and would either have to pass through the narrow waters easily straddled by hostile Air Power, or, as has actually occurred in the present war, be forced to make the long journey round the Cape, in order to reach their destination.

The effort entailed by these operations is out of all proportion to their value to the Empire, and constitutes a great drain on our resources.

Apart from the strategic liabilities, the controversial nature of the task has involved us in endless difficulties with both Jews and Arabs.

IX.

The *motif* underlying our foreign policy became evident soon after the Great War, when it shewed a firm determination to align itself with that of the United States, whose outlook on world affairs is very different from our own. No fault can be found with this policy as a general thesis, but, in practice, it has been carried much too far, to the detriment of our own security. The United States have never been willing to assume any strategical commitments corresponding to political engagements. Under pressure their Government take refuge behind the constitution, which precludes such arrangements; or else the Monroe doctrine can be invoked.

The earliest indication of the future direction of our foreign policy can be found in Mr. Lloyd George's Memoirs, in which he quotes the minutes of Cabinet Meetings; rather a novel procedure.

At one of these meetings, Lord Reading, who had been recently High Commissioner and Ambassador in the United States during the war, formulated this essential liaison with America, which was generally approved by the rest of the Cabinet. The hand of Judmas was plainly visible in this political orientation, and its headquarters were gradually being established on the other side of the Atlantic, in readiness for the next move.

In practical application this policy displayed a determination to do nothing that might run counter to the wishes of the rich and powerful United States, almost amounting to slavish acquiescence in these wishes. The protagonists of this policy always defended it on the grounds of wealth. "America is so rich, she can do anything she pleases."

Wealth. Gross materialism was the most dangerous factor that was undermining our national characteristics of sturdy independence and self-reliance, which had gone far to achieve our great position in the world. Wealth. Always wealth. There was never any mention of that all-important factor in a nation's continued existence and prosperity—its soul.

FROM ADMIRAL TO CABIN BOY

We were occupied in bartering our soul for gold: under the direction of Judmas the pound sterling and the almighty dollar were engaged in a conspiracy to obtain financial control of the whole world.

The further we were drawn into this policy, the greater became our estrangement from some of the European nations who had suffered as a result of the Great War, and had seen the error of their financial ways, and were busily engaged in trying to amend them.

X.

And this talk of souls brings me to my next topic—Ireland—for Ireland still possesses a soul, and Ireland is intimately connected with our strategic security.

Towards the end of 1921 the Irish Treaty was being patched up, after the Irish Republican Army, the Black and Tans, and the Royal Irish Constabulary Auxiliaries, had had their murderous interlude. Decent people in both countries were sick of the sight of this political folly, and the resulting atrocities committed on both sides, and were only too anxious to see agreement reached. Fortunately the politicians were in the same frame of mind, but, in their case, the main motive was to remove any disharmonies that might upset the Washington Naval Conference which was just about to open, and to which delegations from the British Empire had been invited by President Harding.

The United States, with their powerful political Irish faction, had always been inclined to busybody over Irish affairs, and had supplied much assistance to the disaffected in the past.

A statesmanlike settlement of the Irish question in the early years of the present century would have established Irish unity, whilst at the same time giving us access to ports and airfields essential to our mutual success in time of war. We should have found in Ireland a loyal partner, with this quality increasing as the years passed by, and old grievances faded into the mists of the past.

This happy solution was too much to expect from a British Government whose countrymen were rapidly losing their spiritual values in the feverish pursuit of material wealth. All the finer qualities of the human mind had given place to the baser material factors which decided policy in most cases.

The intense desire of the majority of Irish people to see their beloved country united under its own Government was never given full weight in British political circles. Men like Parnell and his followers were never understood at Westminster, where they were regarded merely as pawns in the greater game of British party politics. When one talks to a man like Cahir Healy, of whom I saw a good deal in Brixton Prison, one realises the full extent to which the real Irish nationalist is selflessly sacrificing his whole time and health in the cause which to him is just the be-all and end-all of his existence. A man of this type soars in spiritual value above the ordinary party politician like an eagle above carrion crows. Yet the eagle is kept beating his wings against prison bars, and is regarded as a confounded nuisance by the carrion crows, who remain free to pollute our public life. Some day the reckoning will have to be paid for this reckless pursuit of wealth.

Incidentally Morrison shewed his ignorance of the Irish character by putting Healy in the jug. The latter refused to have anything to do with the Advisory Committee, and had to be let out eventually as an unprofitable asset. On his return to Ireland, his political shares had soared, due to his unjust incarceration by the English, who would have done better from their own point of view, to have let him alone.

During the late summer of 1920 when Terence MacSwiney, the Lord Mayor of Cork, another great single-hearted patriot, was lying in Brixton Prison undergoing the hunger strike which lasted over seventy days and resulted finally in his death, he tried to explain to Dr. Higson, one of the medical officers who looked after him, why he was prepared to die for his principles, and finished up by saying:—"Oh, how we ought to pity the Sassenachs! Their Empire is not only tottering but visibly falling. And once they are down they will never rise. They have no ideals. Their death as a nation will be an eternal one. Thanks be to God, we are Irish."

It will be for us to prove after this calamitous war. that this great—or misguided—man, according to the point of view, was wrong, and that we can emerge from our chastening experience with a soul reborn through the blood, sweat, toil and tears ordained by our politicians, and attain to greater heights than ever before. This happy consummation will require very different guidance to that which we have experienced during the last century of 'progress,' into certain aspects of which we will take a peep presently.

After the Great War, the political atmosphere between England and Ireland had still further deteriorated, and it was unlikely that a satisfactory solution of this important strategic question could be reached in 1921.

There is one particular aspect of this matter which it is desirable to place on record.

Ireland straddles the approaches from the outer seas to the United Kingdom, and is an essential geographical feature of any defence system. Ireland firmly held by an enemy, would form a stranglehold on British communications.

The Irish delegation were very anxious to get rid of all British military occupation in the future Free State as soon as possible. I attended the meetings when naval matters were under discussion as assistant to Lord Beatty, the First Sea Lord.

Mr. Churchill was in the chair, and Michael Collins and Erskine Childers were the Irish representatives.

Michael Collins was both wheedling and persistent; Erskine Childers was far too hostile to condescend to wheedling. But Lord Beatty was adamant on the question of the necessity of having the use of certain Irish ports as naval bases in time of war, which had to be garrisoned accordingly.

Indeed this was such an obvious essential that it is difficult to understand how the British Government came to surrender this right in 1938, when the international situation was so highly strained as to render the lien on these bases of far greater importance than when the Treaty was made seventeen years before. It remains an incredible act of short-sighted folly. No temporary advantage could possibly have atoned for this surrender, and when war came, nothing could move Mr. De Valera from his stubborn attitude of neutrality. We had to pay for our lack of generosity to the Irish in the past.

Mr. De Valera refused to view the danger of a German victory through British eyes. He felt that he owed the British nothing: on the contrary. All said and done, a German victory might bring him that Irish unity which he so ardently desired, and which he would never get from Britain, so long as Judmas had a finger in the pie.

Even the cajoleries of Mr. Roosevelt left him cold. However much one may deplore Mr. De Valera's obstinacy and shortsightedness, he must go on record as one of the few consistent statesmen in the world, and must be regarded as an honest man in comparison with some of the political contortionists at Westminster, whose inconsistent policies have led us to this insane gamble with our Empire, with the strategical dice so heavily loaded against us.

Moreover he speaks for the majority of Irishmen, and we must shoulder the major portion of the blame for our past dealings with Ireland, which led to the adoption of this unfortunate attitude by the Irish today.

Lord Chatfield in a letter to *The Times* published on the 4th February, 1942 offered an explanation of the Admiralty attitude to the surrender of the Irish bases in 1938, in which he stated that nobody foresaw the collapse of the French Army.

This statement amazed me, especially as coming from a member of the Government which had embarked upon this colossal folly. One would have expected a little more knowledge about the internal conditions of a prospective ally.

In my little book 'Look to Your Moat' published in 1937, I anticipated the situation in which the French coast would be in German hands, because I realised the rotten state to which the country had been reduced by the Popular Front Government, and the probability of the people cracking under the stress of war. I clothed this belief in more delicate terms, and laid emphasis on our retention of the Irish bases.

The French are a more logical race than the English. In the years immediately following the Great War, whilst Germany was still in a state of moral collapse and disarmament, there were several occasions upon which the French Government wished to enter the country and enforce the terms of the Peace Treaty. The British Government refused to take part in any such adventures, and were busily engaged in trying to put Germany on her feet again, by financial aid and other means.

There were occasions such as the French occupation of the Ruhr, when relations with France were very strained in consequence. Enforcement of any practical claims against Germany at this time would have been feasible.

After the arrival of Hitler and the impetus thereby given to German rearmament, British policy changed under the guidance of Judmas, which disliked both the German treatment of the Jews, and the German new economic doctrine which threatened the reign of Gold.

Many of the logical French had also changed their views, and preferred a policy of collaboration with their powerful neighbour, whom they had got for keeps, to the risk of the calamity of another war on a falling birthrate and a disunited people, torn with political controversy.

Surely a more intelligible policy than our own. However Judmas and the British politicians prevailed, and France was dragged reluctantly on to the field of battle.

Not much was to be expected from such a start, and there were many in this country, in spite of what Lord Chatfield says, who anticipated the collapse of France at the first severe blow. The quietude of the early months of the war whilst Poland, the bait, was being digested, was deceptive.

Then came Norway, Holland—*puis le déluge*. We have got rather far from the Irish bases: *revenons à nos moutons*.

XI.

The next matter to cause me grave concern was the termination of the Anglo-Japanese Alliance, notice of which was given by the British Government, at about the time the Washington Conference was convened in 1921.

The "Encyclopaedia Britannica" comments upon the final abrogation of the Treaty in 1923 as follows:—

"For twenty-one years it had been the most stable influence in the Far Eastern position, and a cardinal factor in British and Japanese policy."

At the time many people failed to realise the importance of this step, which was lost to sight in all the blah-blah surrounding the Naval Conference, with its accompanying Multiple Power Treaties for dealing with matters in the Far East. These Treaties were not worth the paper they were written on, as far as affording any sense of security went.

Judmas was in such full blast explaining their advantages over a mere bi-lateral Treaty, that the ordinary reader may be excused for missing the significance of the changed conditions. This matter must be discussed at some length because it was the main danger signal pointing out the perils of the path we were beginning to tread, a path obscured by League of Nations' ideals, and beset by very real dangers to the British Empire.

In years gone by whilst we were actively engaged in increasing our territorial possessions in the Far East, no naval threat to supremacy in those waters existed.

Both Australia and New Zealand were immune from attack.

Eighty odd years ago, Japan made her first bow to the world as an aspirant to the ranks of the Great Powers.

By the beginning of the present century she had, under British guidance, made a big advance towards becoming a Naval Power. In 1902, more far-sighted statesmen than any of those who have directed our affairs since the Great War, made a Treaty with Japan, which was increased to an Alliance in 1905.

This instrument provided for the safeguarding of our mutual interests in Eastern Asia and India. Our main object was to provide for the security of our possessions in the Western Pacific, so that we could withdraw most of our naval forces from those waters, and concentrate them at home to meet the growing menace of the Kaiser's new fleet.

The arrangement was welcomed by the Japanese as a sure indication of their growing prestige, and was a valuable asset to them in their victorious war against Russia, which broke out in 1904.

In consequence of the Treaty, the Japanese entered readily into the Great War on 23rd August, 1914, and loyally observed their obligations. Some of their ships travelled as far as the Mediterranean on escort duty, in relief of our fully-extended naval forces.

The Alliance was welcomed by all well-informed people in this country as a factor of the utmost importance in the promotion of our interests in Pacific waters.

At the conclusion of the Great War, the Admiralty took stock of our naval positions all round the world. By this time Japan had reached the status of a first-class Naval Power.

This factor necessitated measures being taken to protect the British Empire against Japanese attack.

However cordial our relations at the time, it would have been highly imprudent to neglect precautions against their deterioration. Treaties and Alliances can be abrogated in a very much shorter time than is required to construct naval bases, and at this time we possessed no naval base in the Pacific capable of accommodating a modern fleet.

The naval leviathans of today require immense preparations to ensure their being valeted satisfactorily in harbour. Docking, fuelling, and repair facilities of this nature were totally lacking, and it would have been impossible to transfer a fleet to the Pacific until these arrangements were perfected. In short, as Mr. Micawber would say, the fleet was immobilised for lack of accommodation and maintenance facilities.

I was surprised at the shock exhibited by the Government when the Admiralty apprised them of the full extent of our lack of readiness in the Far East. Pre-occupation in the events in Home waters during the last two decades had blunted their sensibilities to the rapid growth of Japanese Naval Power. When they realised that our fleet was, to all intents and purposes, anchored to our shores, through lack of intermediate fuelling stations and terminal naval bases, the blood of their great forbears who built our Empire coursed more rapidly through their veins, at the exposure of our impotence. At any rate, after a thorough examination of the matter from a defence viewpoint, a decision was reached to construct a modern naval base at Singapore, as soon as the plans could be prepared.

XII.

When a *post mortem* is held on this war, a great deal of criticism will be heard of the choice of Singapore as a base, in defence of those whose muddled minds lost it. A few remarks may therefore be appropriate.

First and foremost, Singapore was never intended as an operational base against Japan, which is roughly three thousand miles distant: much too far for attacking successfully an enemy in his own Home Waters.

A Fleet operational base today must be as near the enemy shores as is consistent with reasonable immunity for the fleet from air attack when in harbour. Before the days of aircraft, such a fleet base could not be too near the enemy bases. Naval strategy demands that the main battle fleet shall be in a position whence it can attack the enemy's battle fleet, before the latter can raid the sea communications which it is necessary to keep open. The battle fleet must therefore be stationed in advance of its own vital waterways, so that these can be safely used by merchant vessels, and the smaller and less powerful classes of war vessels employed in protecting them.

This is the essence of naval strategy, and the closer to the foe the battle fleet can lie in wait the better. But since the advent of air attack, it is not possible to maintain the fleet at an anchorage exposed to heavy attack by land-based aircraft. The main fleets have therefore been driven apart to the extent of several hundred miles, and this distance will increase as air power becomes progressively more formidable, unless the air defences improve, so as to keep pace with the scale of attack.

Such progress in anti-aircraft defence is not in sight, due to the mobility of aircraft, which is exceedingly difficult to counter. Indeed, every day the operation of warships within reach of land-based enemy aircraft becomes more hazardous, until one begins to wonder naturally whether the fleet is really required, or whether it has not been rendered obsolete by the air. Such a contention does not bear investigation. So long as merchant ships ply the seas carrying the world's trade, so long will fighting ships be needed to protect them, against attack by enemy vessels.

Large areas of ocean are unattainable by land-based aircraft, nor can these work continuously and efficiently in all conditions, especially in fog, tempestuous weather, and at night.

If the day ever arrives when aircraft can replace ships as carriers of the world's trade, then fleets will pass automatically out of commission.

Today, it is hard to imagine such a condition of affairs, in view of the vast bulk of the world's traffic. The force of gravity is a powerful deterrent to lifting this mass of material into the air, and the mind boggles at the thought of the number and size of the necessary transport machines. However we have seen so many wonders in our own day, that such an eventuality cannot be ruled out as impossible.

We are dealing here with the present time and its immediate future, which involves ships as the primary transporters of overseas goods. Therefore navies must continue to function under the increasing handicap of air developments, demanding elaborate air protection for the fleet itself.

XIII.

A fleet operational base of the nature we have just discussed, is not available today against Japan, whose shores are remote from any naval base we are in a position to establish.

Singapore is admirably sited as the base for a fleet intended to protect our possessions, with the exception of Hong Kong, from attack by Japan. No Japanese forces contemplating attack on Australia or New Zealand, or an advance into the Indian Ocean, could possibly afford to make the attempt whilst leaving a powerful fleet on its flank at Singapore. But the fleet must be there. That is the whole essence of the matter.

A base without a fleet is like a kennel without a watch-dog, or a deserted hornet's nest. Moreover it is a liability, not an asset: it needs defence whilst robbed of its prime source of defence—the fleet.

Had the new fleet base in the Far East been sited in Australia, as many advocated, possibly it would have been easier to defend, but the sea approaches to India and Africa would have been left uncovered.

Hong Kong would have been an even better site than Singapore for a naval base to deter a Japanese advance southward, but an examination of its defence possibilities soon rendered the idea impracticable. Moreover, under the agreement reached at the Washington Conference, further development of a naval base at Hong Kong was forbidden: of this more anon.

The defence requirements of our oversea territories have always been calculated on a well-considered plan, by which the maximum scale of attack which a possible adversary can mount, before the fleet arrives on the scene to prevent further oversea movement of enemy forces, is met by the local defence forces necessary to hold the fort during this hiatus. This interval is known technically as the Period before Relief.

Naturally this period lengthens with the distance of the base from Home Waters. Worked out in this manner, the size of the garrison necessary to render Hong Kong secure was beyond the bounds of practical politics, and it is obviously of no use to construct an important and costly naval base, unless it is reasonably safe.

Singapore was regarded as secure with a comparatively modest garrison, but the military and air advisers greatly under-estimated the possibilities of land attack via the Malay States; a difficult region of swamp and jungle.

FROM ADMIRAL TO CABIN BOY

History has proved the falsity of the defence calculations, but, in fairness, it must be said that the Government were the real culprits. No prevision could have contemplated the Japanese being given a free hand to land when and where they chose all over the Malay Peninsula, without interference from our naval forces.

These enemy attacks were rendered possible by the Japanese occupation of French Indo-China before the outbreak of the Japanese war, another circumstance which no military advisers could have been expected to anticipate.

As it was, the Japs could operate in front, flank, or rear of our defence forces in the Malay States, and no gallantly could have availed against such a handicap.

Had the fleet been at Singapore in adequate strength, no enemy overseas forces could have landed to attack: it is highly probable that the Japanese would never have attempted to carry the war into the Southern hemisphere.

When Singapore was chosen as the main naval base in Far Eastern waters, it was fully realised that it could only be regarded as a fleet assembly and repair base in the best available site for defending our possessions in the Far East against attack by Japan. It was in no way a threat to Japan, against whom we harboured no aggressive plans.

XIV.

So much for the choice of Singapore. At about the same time as this decision was reached, the British Government elected to serve notice of the termination of the Anglo-Japanese Alliance. The principal reason for this decision was the hostility of the United States to this alliance, and it will be remembered that the main plank in our new foreign policy, was the firm intention to work in friendly collaboration with the United States. The Washington Naval Conference was approaching, and the politicians wished to enter these discussions with no avoidable clouds on the horizon.

There were other considerations, it is true: doubt existed as to whether the Treaty was in keeping with the new era of international collaboration introduced by the League Covenant: Canada was inclined to take the same view as America, and both Australia and New Zealand harboured doubts as to the value of the Treaty, which were distinctly short-sighted on their part. On the other hand all the Departments of the British Government which were consulted, were in favour of the continuance of the Treaty, with the exception of the Foreign Office, which has, naturally, the biggest say in a matter of foreign policy. And so this decision, big with the fate of the British Empire, was taken. Japanese pride was extremely hurt at the sudden and unexpected notice to terminate the Treaty by whose existence Japanese prestige had been greatly enhanced. There was also considerable bewilderment as to the design behind British action. The Japanese had not taken kindly to the Genevan idea of "All the world a happy family," and were far from content with their younger son's portion, which could have been increased more easily with the British Alliance still in force: at least, so they thought.

The Japanese had behaved loyally to the terms of the Alliance, and although it would have been put to a severe test by the acquisitive nature of the Japanese longterm foreign policy, we could have kept a restraining hand on this policy with far greater effect than has been possible since the termination of the Treaty, and the consequent deterioration of our friendly relations. Our motives for abrogating the Treaty were never fully understood or trusted, and suspicion increased with the passage of the years, which shewed our subservience to American policy to an ever increasing extent.

XV.

The upshot of the Washington Naval Conference was a further handicap to our influence and strategic position in the Far East. The nations represented at this conference were the United States, the British Empire, Japan, France and Italy.

The Americans were only interested in the British Empire and Japan. Their original proposals, announced with dramatic surprise at the opening meeting, made no mention of France and Italy. Their principal object was to fix the strength of the Japanese Navy at three-fifths of the forces allotted to the United States or the British Empire, between whom parity was suggested, and accepted in principle by Lord Balfour, the head of the British delegation. As a matter of fact he received his peerage just after the Conference.

The Japanese were much perturbed at these proposals, which gave them a smaller ration than they were prepared to accept, and a long delay ensued, at the end of which they countered with a neat proposition of their own. They announced that they would only be willing to accept the modest quantum suggested, provided that the Powers signatory to the Treaty would agree to leave all their naval bases within a certain radius of Japan in their existing state of development, that is to say *in statu quo.*

As none of these bases is capable of maintaining a modern fleet, this proposal, which the Japanese considered essential to their security, amounted to an invitation to the other countries to be content with obsolete naval establishments in the waters included under the ban.

The Americans had been busily protesting their pacific intentions in regard to the rest of the world, and could not reasonably object to this restriction on the movements of their modern warships on political grounds. American naval officers were fully alive to the insidious nature of this wily proposal, and pointed out that a fleet which could not be moved about at will, ceased to be an instrument of diplomatic pressure if occasion arose, or of war-like potency if hostilities eventuated. President Harding's Government were so keen on the success of their "Arms Parley," that they ignored the protests of their naval experts, and accepted the Japanese view. This was a tremendous score for the Japs.

To all intents and purposes, the American fleet was incapable of operating in the Western Pacific for the duration of the Treaty, as the naval base at Manila was included.

We had to throw in Hong Kong, but this was not a matter of great moment, as it had been decided already that Hong Kong could not be relied upon as our main naval base in Pacific Waters, on account of the practical impossibility of providing adequate defences.

Singapore lay outside the prohibited radius: we were very firm about this, and the Japs never pressed the point, but only referred to it jokingly. Our case was a strong one, as no flight of imagination could regard the establishment of this base as other than a defensive measure.

The Japanese departed from Washington after achieving a great strategic triumph, which left them masters of the Western Pacific. The American fleet was virtually tethered to its own shores, although eventually Pearl Harbour was developed as an outlying base in mid-ocean. Even this vantage point was much too far from Japan to be used as a base for offensive strategy in the event of war.

This fact, coupled with the parochial views on naval strategy held in the United States, made me realise that, in any conflict with Japan, we should be playing a lone hand, under immense disadvantages of distance from our main fleet bases in Home waters.

In the days to come, as the Eastern Dominions of our Empire grew and prospered, it was conceivable that they might maintain their own fleet at Singapore. In the meantime, the main responsibility for the protection of the Empire in the Far East remained in the hands of the British Government at home.

If, as seemed highly probable, Japan cherished aggressive ambitions to the southward, it was unlikely that she would be so accommodating as to wait for a re-disposition of our naval strength, adversely affecting her own position.

Yet this was the moment chosen to part with any restraining influence we might have exercised over Japanese designs, by virtue of the Alliance.

This was a major error in post-war diplomacy for which we have paid bitterly: unfortunately it does not stand alone.

We have often committed mistakes in the past, but never have we concentrated so many into such a short period of time, as in the two decades after the Great War.

FROM ADMIRAL TO CABIN BOY

A Foreign Policy that neglects strategical conditions is bound to come to grief in the long run, and we shall see that our foreign policy during the period under consideration resulted in the estrangement of those countries whose friendship was essential to our own security, and in their ultimate combination against us, whereby they achieved a Collective Security far in advance of any attained by its sponsors at Geneva. Our anxiety to curry favour with our rich relations across the Atlantic was costing us dear.

The American objections to the Anglo-Japanese Alliance were, to say the least, short-sighted. The United States Government should have been only too pleased at any restraining influence placed on the land of the Rising Sun by an Alliance which could never have been used against themselves.

However Judmas and other powerful influences thought differently. We exchanged the substance of the Anglo-Japanese Alliance for the shadow of some valueless multi-lateral pacts, and did an incalculable amount of harm to our interests in the Far East.

It is improbable that a continuation of the Alliance would have called a halt to Japan's long-term policy of expansion in the western Pacific: far from it. But Japan was proud of the Alliance, fully alive to its advantages, and would have been careful to avoid any abrupt severance of its ties by violent action. The Yellow Peril would have remained in the background, instead of being very much to the fore, as it is today.

XVI.

One interesting little happening in connection with the Washington Conference throws a light on the character of Winston Churchill, and shews that he was not always such a champion of the efficient state of our defence forces.

When, at a later date, the Press went to all lengths to boost Churchill into Chamberlain's shoes, one of the principal factors advocated in his favour, was that he had always been a stout upholder of our main pillar of defence, the British Navy. *Autres temps, autres moeurs.*

At the time of which we are speaking, Churchill was Secretary of State for the Colonies, in Mr. Lloyd George's National Government.

At Washington one day, Mr. Balfour received a telegram from Downing Street, stating that the Government were much perturbed to hear that the naval members of our Delegation at Washington were doing their best to defeat one of the American proposals which was dear to the heart of the British Government, namely the ten years' building holiday for Capital ships.

Mr. Balfour was instructed to caution them accordingly, and we were all made to feel rather dirty dogs, by the wording of the message.

Mr. Balfour was very indignant at receiving such a communication, which was based upon hearsay, besides being most insulting to Lord Beatty and his naval assistants.

It is quite true that we regarded this proposal as harmful to our interests, as a country whose navy was all-important, though not apparently to politicians.

Without going into too much detail, the construction of big battleships requires the employment of certain highly technical industries, such as the manufacture of armour plate, whose plant could not be diverted to other uses. The Firms concerned would therefore have to be closed down, or subsidised in idleness. This suggested hiatus coming at a time when the dearly-bought lessons of the recent war required to be applied and tested by incorporation in new ships, was a serious handicap to our naval technicians, whose unrivalled experience was relied upon, to keep us in the van of shipbuilding progress.

The naval Delegation had carried their anxieties no further than was their bounden duty, in pointing out both to Mr. Balfour and the Board of Admiralty, the naval disadvantages of the proposal.

The whole thing was a typical foreign dodge for putting our naval supremacy in fetters, and we felt much injured that our own Government should treat our valid objections as disloyalty. However, there it was, Mr. Balfour expostulated mildly with Lloyd George, and the matter dropped.

Shortly afterwards, Lord Beatty returned to England in advance of the remainder, and took the opportunity to attend a Defence Meeting as soon as he could. He claimed priority for the discussion of this insulting message, over other business.

Lloyd George was absent, and Churchill was in the Chair. The latter endeavoured to postpone discussion on the plea that the Prime Minister's reproof could not be considered in his absence. Lord Beatty was adamant; it was always a treat to see him at grips with the politicians: L.G., and probably others, disliked him on this account. He was a match for them, and this was not expected of generals and admirals.

So the telegram was discussed, and it turned out that Churchill had drafted the offending message himself, although he claimed to have shewn it to other members of the Cabinet. We received a belated tribute to our merits, thanks entirely to the firm stand adopted by Lord Beatty.

At a later date, Churchill was once more to encroach upon the functions of the Prime Minister, by carrying on a clandestine correspondence with the President of the United States, under the pseudonym of 'Naval Person.' These messages were passed via the American Embassy in London, during the early days of the second or Greater War in 1939.

Captain Ramsay, the Member for South Midlothian and Peebles, became aware of this correspondence, which was being carried out behind Mr. Neville Chamberlain's back, although Mr. Churchill has assured us that it was with his knowledge. Ramsay was considering his correct action in the matter, when Churchill succeeded to the office of Prime Minister, and the gallant member was popped into Brixton Prison out of harm's way. Churchill was on firmer ground on this latter occasion, as he was already the heir apparent by general acclaim.

One of my colleagues at Brixton Prison was *maître d'hôtel* at the Savoy, and he had an interesting tale of constant dinner parties in a private room at which Lord Southwood, Lord Bearsted, Sir John Ellerman, Mr. Israel Moses Sieff and Mr. Churchill, generally formed the company. Possibly a great deal of the inner history of England during these stirring times would have been gleaned by any eavesdropper at these convivial little parties of 'British' leaders.

XVII.

The Washington Conference was a success in many respects, apart from the adverse situation in the Far East. In Europe our Foreign Policy centred round the League of Nations, which was regarded as a panacea for the world's ills. Geneva became a hotbed of international intrigue.

Our attitude to Germany during the first decade after the war, was by no means hostile; rather paternal and advisory. Germany resembled a pupil in a kind of political Borstal institution, the object of which was to try and rescue youthful political criminals, and guide them into a wise democratic future.

This suited Judmas nicely, and there were many pickings to be had. Money flowed into Germany and Eastern Europe, which was still in a state of political and economic chaos: money which was badly needed for the development and strengthening of the British Empire was deflected to lands where the dividends were likely to be quicker to return, and larger in extent.

The profits from cheap industry in Poland were more satisfactory than those that would have been obtained by blazing a new trail in our Dominions and Colonies.

XVIII.

The uneasy 1920's passed away with much international bickering, including several abortive conferences on disarmament, at which the principal 'successes' were gained by a further clipping of Britain's naval wings.

Our politicians—I cannot bring myself to call them statesmen—had acquired a cheap popularity at home by the savings effected at the Washington Conference. They found it easier to shew outward and visible signs of further 'successes' by continuing to mortgage our naval security, rather than by reaching international agreement on the size of military establishments and air forces, which could be more readily camouflaged by unscrupulous signatories.

Battleships and submarines cannot be produced from the sleeve or the conjuror's hat; they require a considerable period for gestation.

The United States took the lead in most of these proposals, and we followed obsequiously in their wake. These were anxious times for those who loved their country, and did not relish the risk to its security which the Westminster mountebanks were taking with such apparent satisfaction to themselves. Trouble was seething in all directions. It became palpable to the ordinary individual that further war would result unless some real attempt were made to settle international differences.

There were many recipes for avoiding war. Disarmament was the prescription favoured by Mr. Arthur Henderson and other muddle-headed idealists. Take away their arms and they cannot fight. Only the most feeble efforts were made to reconcile the crying injustices calling for treatment at Geneva by the dope doctors. No; the cart must come before the horse; disarmament before justice; folly before wisdom. It was heartbreaking to watch all the advantages we had gained by winning the Great War, being frittered away by the ineptitude of corrupt or misguided politicians.

XIX.

In 1931 Japan stirred things up by walking into Manchuria, the home of much foreign investment, in pursuit of her long-term policy of economic development, and in order to secure an air frontier more distant from her vulnerable home islands; such a frontier as would be welcome to us, if obtainable.

This started the bees at Geneva swarming in full cluster. Meetings were held all over this country calling for vengeance on this desecrator of League principles.

The Church led the hue and cry with true Christian zeal: the valour of ignorance. Dr. Lang, then Archbishop of Canterbury, took the chair at a bumper meeting at the Albert Hall calling for sanctions against Japan.

His gaiters swelled with righteous wrath: his head with episcopal folly.

Why do not these pillars of the Church take the trouble to discover what is entailed by the policies they advocate so airily? Much harm is done by threatening something that cannot be performed, even with the full support of political clerics. Our latter-day Bishops have done the Church an untold amount of harm, by their foolish dabbling in political matters entailing military measures far beyond their ken.

Apart from the Church leaders, I am quite sure that none of the professors, pressmen and political pundits, had any idea of the inevitable consequences of following their advice.

They did not realise that sanctions were only a form of pressure that must have resulted in war, unless the unlikely happened, and the offending country toed the line in obedience to the threats thundered at her from Geneva.

It was most improbable that the fiery national spirit of Japan would be quenched by the blasts of a group of scheming politicians many thousands of miles away: hardly worth gambling upon, when a negative result would involve such a heavy loss of 'face..' Or were the enthusiastic supporters of sanctions ready to go to the lengths of war? And, if so, had they the foggiest idea of the enormous effort entailed in making war at the other side of the world? And who would supply the necessary League Forces? In the end wiser counsels prevailed, and an attempt was made to save 'face' after all the hullabaloo, by the dispatch of the inevitable commission under the aegis of Lord Lytton, which wrote the inevitably ponderous report, as a result of its brief sojourn in the disputed area. This report suffered the customary doom of all such compilations, in that few read it, and none took any action upon it.

It is possible that the Japanese felt that they knew more about Manchuria than the members of the Commission, and may have wondered mildly whether their own interference in the affairs of a western land such as Ireland, would have been received with any greater respect.

FROM ADMIRAL TO CABIN BOY

Thus ended the first big-scale threat from the West to coerce the East, which had grown up so rapidly that it had achieved manhood, whilst Europe was rapidly lapsing into its second childhood.

The 'lean and slippered pantaloon' in the West was shortly to be given a painful education by the Eastern soldier 'sudden and quick in quarrel.'

Needless to say, foremost among the windy demagogues shouting for vengeance was to be found our leading amateur strategist Winston Churchill, who was at that time out of favour with the political figures strutting on the national stage, and had to content himself with pulling a few unofficial strings behind the wings.

XX.

In 1933 Adolf Hitler achieved power in Germany, and upset the whole of the stage setting, so admirably arranged by Judmas. This remarkable man was fully alive to the evil potentialities of Judmas, and was determined to remove its influence in European affairs.

Unfortunately he was in a hurry: also, being German, he handled his foes within the State tactlessly and cruelly with little regard to foreign opinion, thus raising an unnecessary number of enemies, and obscuring his good qualities and real greatness. Judmas took immediate alarm, and from that time onwards our foreign policy commenced its re-orientation against Germany, although, at first, the outward and visible signs were not very clear.

Gradually, however, the National Press, with the assistance of Judmas, began to distort all the news coming out of Germany, giving it a sinister twist.

Of course Hitler himself came in for the worst of it: Hitler the paper-hanger: Hitler the rug-biter. I could not help feeling sometimes that if Hitler could produce such striking results on a diet of rugs, our Mr. Baldwin might have given a trial to the system, through the medium of the whole carpet stock of Maple's and Hampton's emporia, and even Mr. Churchill might have been improved by chewing a couple of Persian rugs occasionally.

I paid my first visit to Germany in 1935, and nobody with any powers of observation at all, could have helped being struck by the gross discrepancy between the facts of daily life in Germany, and their warped representation to the British public by their Daily Press.

It was incredible that such a complete metamorphosis could have taken place so soon after the advent of the new régime, as we were being led to believe.

Whole nations do not change their characteristics in this fashion; something was very wrong somewhere.

It was a great shock to me, and brought home, as nothing else could have done, the power for evil of the hidden forces which were at work to create a deterioration in the friendly relations between two great countries, upon whom the peace of the whole world depended, to say nothing of our own prosperity.

At this time I had not succeeded in getting Judmas into proper focus, and I was greatly mystified by the discrepancy between fact and fiction, as served up to British breakfast tables.

No restrictions were placed on travel or conversation in Germany; everywhere I received a kind and genuinely friendly welcome, and there was no doubt of the sincerity of the many people I met, for an amicable settlement of outstanding differences with England, and the re-commencement of an era of friendly relations.

There was so much to be gained by wise action in this direction on the part of the politicians of both nations. But time was short; the sands were running out, and there were many trying to hasten the advent of Mars.

XXI.

Soon after the Nazi Régime succeeded to power, Mussolini threw a spanner into the world's gear-box, by announcing his projected rape of Abyssinia.

Once more League circles were a-flutter: here was a full-blooded member proposing to break the Club Rules by attacking a smaller Colleague.

The shock was as great as that which would have been

FROM ADMIRAL TO CABIN BOY

caused in the smoking-room of the Athenaeum, if an Anglican Bishop had strolled across the floor, and brought a straight left to the chin of one of his smaller and darker brethren.

This is no place to argue the rights and wrongs of the Italian dictator's project: enough to say that both were present, as in nearly every dispute. My only object is to point out the folly of our attitude in the matter, by which we made certain of a new enemy in the hub of our sea-communications in the Mediterranean: aforesaid enemy having been bound to us hitherto by ties of interest and gratitude.

"Quem Deus vult perdere, prius dementat," and the reference is not to Mussolini but to John Bull.

This was the first appearance in heavy drama of one of our new actors, Mr. Anthony Eden, a prime favourite with the International Politicians, who had been put through a lengthy course of study in their subtle methods at Geneva, and must have passed with honours, as he was written up so heartily in the Press. Later on, he was to play a still more important part as one of the leading members of the British Empire Demolition Squad at Westminster, during the war which was rapidly approaching.

Sir Samuel Hoare* was Secretary of State for Foreign Affairs when the incident started. He behaved on this occasion with unusual insight, by collaborating with his French Colleague, Pierre Laval, in arranging a *modus vivendi* which would have satisfied the Roman Caesar, although perhaps hardly up to the highest standard of League ideals.

However they had reckoned without Judmas, who had a grudge against Musso. The news leaked out too soon, before the stage was properly set for the *détente,* and the British national Press, in compliance with its Master's voice, rent the proposed agreement in pieces. A weeping Sam vacated his chair in Downing Street, and retired to an obscurity, whence I hoped he would never return.

Debonair Anthony stepped into his shoes, and read the Riot Act to an apoplectic Mussolini, threatening him with economic sanctions of a drastic nature, much to the

---

* Now Lord Templewood.

perturbation of some of his colleagues at Geneva, especially those whose countries were small and unpleasantly close to the angry man of Rome.

However Laval tipped off his friend Mussolini that the British would not go to war over this imbroglio, so Mussolini was enabled to announce boldly that the threatened oil sanction would mean war. This led to hasty recession at Geneva, and only some face-saving sanctions of smaller importance were imposed on the transgressor.

This policy of half-measures resulted, as all such policies do, in exacerbating Italian sentiment without producing much practical result, other than inconvenience to all parties concerned.

Mussolini took care that his countrymen should not forget this insult to the Roman Eagles, and placarded many public buildings in Italy with an inscription to the effect that on such and such a date, fifty-one nations had administered this snub to Italy: a 'Lest we forget' reminder for all to read.

From that time onwards, Mussolini was definitely aligned with his uncongenial neighbour in Berlin, whom he was still inclined to treat in a high-handed manner, as a member of the Junior School. Incalculable harm was done to our imperial interests by this new menace to an important line of sea-communication. The threat was growing more important every day with the increasing ability of aircraft to interfere with the movements of ships.

The Axis was still unformed, nor had Japan definitely joined the enemies of democracy, but it was becoming more apparent daily, that in the event of an outbreak of war, we should probably find ourselves confronted by the formidable combination of Germany, Italy and Japan, threatening our Empire territories at the eastern and western extremities of the great continent formed by Europe, Asia, and Africa, as well as along the shorter line of communication connecting them, through the Mediterranean. We should only be able to off-set this dangerous trio by France as our sole European ally of any consequence; a France torn by political controversy and corruption, and on that account unlikely to prove a very reliable consort.

The United States would undoubtedly be a friendly neutral, but one situated in a very disadvantageous strategic position, being thousands of miles behind the lines of sea-communication on both the Atlantic and Pacific fronts.

It would be difficult to imagine a more dangerous strategical combination against our Empire, and yet this was the achievement of our foreign policy in the period between the two wars, optimistically referred to as 'Unfinished Victory' by Arthur Bryant. He does not seem to have realised that the strategic scales had become so heavily weighted against us in the interval, that even ostensible military victory in a further war, would entail defeat in reality, so far as our position as a World Power went: others would reap the benefit, in accordance with the Judmas plan.

Looking back, and being wise after the event, much tribulation might have been saved if the Italian bluff had been called at the time of the Abyssinian crisis, even if we had been the sole contributor to the Collective Security bag.

There were many reasons against this policy: the fallacy of Collective Security would have been exposed, and our politicians were feeling a bit weak about the knees, as a result of letting down our armed forces so badly during the last few years. Sitting over the Suez Canal, we were in a strong position to say 'No' to the Duce, but, here again, as the strongest naval Power, we did not wish to infringe the Suez Canal Convention, which was of great consequence to ourselves.

Still the might-have-been is always a tantalising thought. My own view is that the major crisis would only have been postponed, not averted, although when it had eventually come, we should have started in a more advantageous position.

XXII.

The Civil War in Spain opened my eyes finally to the hidden powers of evil which were upsetting the world.

Spain was the next victim selected for Communism by Judmas. The soi-disant elected Government of

Spain received the full backing of Communist Russia, whilst Italy and Germany openly supported the 'rebels' under General Franco, representing a strong nationalist and Catholic movement.

France gave half-hearted support to the Judmas candidate in this fratricidal struggle: we gave no active assistance, but the national Press was mobilised in favour of the existing régime, and its misrepresentation of the causes of the conflict, and of the ebb and flow of the fortunes of war, would have taken a lot of beating in the Fleet Street Ananias Sweepstakes, open to all comers.

It soon became obvious that the Axis Powers were not prepared to see Spain turned into an outpost of Bolshevism and a disciple of Judmas in Western Europe, and the ultimate result of hostilities was never much in doubt.

Had the Democracies been ready and willing to give full support to the Red candidate at this time, the World War Balloon would have gone up three years earlier, catching all the bigger contestants in a state of comparative unpreparedness. If, as subsequently transpired, they were determined to challenge Germany's policy in Europe, this might have been a better moment to do so. I do not know; nobody else knows. All we can say is that when war did come, Hitler was fully prepared and all the remainder were not.

XXIII.

However the Spanish war revealed clearly to me the dangers to our Empire, which beset the path we were treading, with popular feeling inflamed by our national Press. The whole tendency of this campaign was to decry any nationalist symptoms which became visible, and which were highly obnoxious to the new international theories with which it was desired to imbue our intensely insular people: theories beautiful to some in conception, but impracticable to all in reality.

The proud and essentially national revivals we were witnessing in Europe, the upsurge of the national spirit in Germany, Italy, Spain, Portugal, Hungary and so on, were extremely formidable movements, not easily killed by the mawkish summons to internationalism, voiced in the popular Press.

Nationalism must lie at the root of any patriotic endeavour: the herd instinct as opposed to the Zoo instinct of internationalism. Patriotism in its old-fashioned sense, meaning love of one's own country, is the only sentiment to which people will respond readily in time of stress.

There is plenty of scope for international co-operation without trying to kill the healthy national feelings, which every individual should be proud to exhibit.

There is nothing in such feelings that need interfere in any way with the development of the closest friendship and mutual assistance between nations: on the contrary, they should help to foster good relations in a worthy spirit of emulation.

However nationalist symptoms were opposed to the new, sickly, common citizenship-of-the-world ideas which the 'liberal' countries had been trying to foster during the past century. They were also harmful to Judmas ambitions which aim at a world-state controlled by a system of international finance manipulated by Judmas: this is the heaven on earth to which we were being guided, and which these new European developments threatened to upset. These developments were accompanied by new economic theories, which would be a death-blow to the Judmas plan.

The countries involved were determined to break the power of international finance, the activities of which were held responsible for the trade booms and slumps to which we had become accustomed in recent years, with their accompanying miseries of unemployment and want.

The new leaders felt that the system of *laissez-faire* which had been allowed to develop in trade, was too unwieldy to control. They visualised a number of self-contained economic Groups, which could regulate their output and markets in industrial and agricultural commodities, so as to maintain a well-balanced economy, and banish the fear of sudden and uncontrollable factors appearing to disorganise regular employment and prosperity; Napoleon's policy re-incarnated after nearly a century and a half had elapsed since Judmas assisted in giving him the *coup-de-grace*.

The intention was that any requirements in raw materials and finished products, with which the Groups could not supply themselves, were to be obtained by the central organisation of each Group through a scheme of barter with other Groups. It was claimed that such a system would enable countries to develop their natural wealth, and obtain its full value, in addition to a higher standard of living, better than would the existing system, in which the big international financial Houses regulated the supply and cost of money, which had ceased to be a medium of exchange, and had blossomed into a commodity used to beget more of its own substance—money breeding money —without any accompanying increase in real wealth in some form or another.

I am no economist, as anyone who is reading these pages will speedily gather. I have merely tried to give in as few words as possible, the gist of what many wise people today regard as the root of all the trouble and unrest in the world—the Money Power. I can only bring to this subject the modicum of common-sense with which I have been blessed. Within these limits, the new system seems to have much to be said for it.

The natural resources and human labour of each country would be employed to much greater advantage than when operating under the handicap of an artificially-controlled financial system, whose vagaries can never be forecast by producer and consumer, but only by the stage-managers appointed by Judmas.

The thing that appealed to me particularly in the new proposals was the greatly increased prosperity which would be bound to develop in our Empire, when it formed a homogeneous unit in the new system. Many of the handicaps which hamper Empire development today, can be traced to the Money system, which diverts to more profitable channels the resources required for our own Imperial progress.

All this is sheer heresy to Judmas which recognises no territorial limits and respects no human ideals, but regards the whole world as one glorious financial playground to be used for its own benefit. Naturally these objectives are not stated so crudely, but are hidden under a lot of benevolent sentiments, intended to keep the nations quiet and unaware.

XXIV.

At this juncture our national leaders had to make up their minds whether we were in a position to contest the growth of these new policies in Europe and the Far East, whilst at the same time defending our vast Empire.

Strategically speaking, we were in a highly dangerous position, and the stakes we should be playing for in this new clash of rival social and economic theories, would be the whole future existence of our Empire, neither more nor less.

If the Empire disintegrated as a result of the war now getting so unpleasantly close, we should be far worse off than if we had been content to leave Europe to its own devices and to concentrate all our efforts on the defence and development of our great heritage, in the confident hope that the rest of the world would ultimately follow our successful leadership; at the best, the Empire would be sorely shaken.

The policy of non-intervention in Europe would have involved the scrapping of one of the cardinal points in our long-standing foreign policy, by which we had never been prepared to see the hegemony of Europe in the hands of one of its Great Powers.

Most of our wars since Tudor days have been caused by our insistence on preserving the balance of power in Europe. Our foreign policy had remained faithful to this creed, which had had a retarding effect on the peaceful development of our own expanding Dominions. However the Foreign Office still lay under the spell of this ancient shibboleth, and appeared unable to realise that modern conditions demanded a revision.

Our world position today is very different from that of Tudor or Stuart days—or rather it was, before this disastrous war—when we were just a little island lying in the shadow of a great continent. In those days it was distinctly to our advantage to see that Europe did not fall under the domination of any one Power, because we should have been undoubtedly gobbled up in the process. Thus we remained a most disturbing factor in European politics.

It is true that we never landed any large forces on the Continent in defence of our policy, but as we waxed richer under the influence of our growing sea power, we were enabled to subsidise the efforts of other nations more immediately concerned, and hire mercenaries to fight our battles.

Wars were quite gentlemanly affairs in those days before totalitarian theories had introduced the all-in Rules which disgrace the warfare of today, and have debased civilisation to the level of the jungle.

Lord Chatham was probably the greatest exponent of the skillful use of Sea Power in aid of continental war-fare, during the Seven Years War. I should like to have heard his views on his titular successor Churchill, and his boon companions, who have been busily engaged in costly operations all round the compass, in what many people would consider non-British interests, a thing which Pitt so carefully avoided doing.

Instead of concentrating all our efforts on the defence and development of our great Empire, and leaving Europe to achieve its own salvation, we have continued our mischievous interference in European disputes, and overtaxed our strength.

Had we stood aside on this occasion, the fight would probably have developed into a straight fight between Slav and Teuton: the former armed by Judmas, and the latter by his own untiring efforts. Europe would have been kept free from the Asiatic hordes which now threaten it; at least, so I expect.

With the correct distribution of our defence forces in a sound foreign policy, we could have held our Empire unaided, as surely as our ancestors built it, with the exception of certain commitments in the Mediterranean which have been undertaken since the last war, and which would never have been accepted by any Government that knew their job, and were not acting under alien pressure.

We can only hope that, under wiser and more far-seeing leadership in the future, we shall be able to retrieve our position in the world, a position which we shall forfeit temporarily through our own folly, whatever the outcome of the present struggle.

XXV.

By 1937 the strategic line-up in the event of war had become fairly plain: we should find ourselves opposed by one of the most powerful combinations that could threaten our Empire—Germany, Italy and Japan. Although Japan had still not joined the axis, it was clear where her interest and sympathies lay. Against this formidable trio we could only muster a France, whose difficulties have been already mentioned, and the friendly neutrality of the United States. Russia was a doubtful quantity, but the natural foe of Germany.

Germany and Italy would pin our naval forces to Home and Mediterranean waters, and it looked as if there would be little or nothing to spare for the Far East, where the real danger to the Empire lay.

Moreover with Italy in the war, it was quite likely that the Mediterranean would be rendered dangerous to merchant ships and troop transports, through the medium of hostile aircraft. This would necessitate all our traffic bound East of Suez going by the longer sea route round the Cape of Good Hope: furthermore, our operations in the Mediterranean itself, would be much more difficult to supply, reinforce and defend.

It is necessary to bear in mind constantly that the fleet only exists to keep the sea communications open for our ships, and to deny them to the enemy. If our merchant ships are unable to use the waters by reason of aircraft, the main object for which the fleet maintains itself in those waters is gone.

The fleet lying in the enclosed waters of the Mediterranean would be a constant source of anxiety. Malta would be too close to Italy to be healthy as a naval base, and the fleet would be forced back to Alexandria or Gibraltar.

In these circumstances, when the naval bases themselves were our only responsibility in the Mediterranean, it would have been an advantage to have withdrawn the fleet entirely from these waters, with no loss other than prestige. We had done it before in our history, and we could do it again without any permanent loss, as after the war we should return.

But now we had Palestine hanging round our neck, and its defence must entail the keeping open of the Mediterranean, if possible. Mr. Balfour's Declaration had made it morally necessary for us to accept the mandate in the interests of the Jews. The oil was useful too, but only as long as the fleet was in the Mediterranean. For Home purposes, all the oil we need would come by the safer route across the Atlantic from America, which was only slightly longer than the journey from Haifa.

XXVI.

But even if the fleet could be released from its responsibilities in the Mediterranean, we should still be unable to send a fleet to the Far East capable of dealing with the Japanese, so long as we were threatened at home by Germany.

In the absence of such a fleet, the Japanese would be free to carry out their ambitious scheme for expansion to the Southward, which was common knowledge, and to annex the outlying portions of our Empire at their leisure.

If we could not keep in Eastern waters a fleet at least equal to the Japanese naval forces, and this would be the minimum needed for defensive purposes without contemplating the offensive, which would require our whole fleet, it was an absolute certainty that we should be left to gaze in impotence from our distant islands, whilst this rape was in progress.

There was no doubt at all about this matter; it was a hundred percent certainty.

This point must be kept clearly in mind, in order to appreciate the fatuity of our political leaders, who insisted on embroiling the Empire in European affairs, which did not directly concern us, whilst they left our own real danger spot entirely unprotected, or at any rate, quite inadequately protected.

And the thing was so crystal clear, that any child who could count up to ten, could have grasped this simple truth; it simply stared us in the face.

And the only way in which we could release the fleet for employment in the threatened area, was by remaining on good terms with Germany, or, better still, by entering into a firm alliance. This would only have been possible, if we had given up our perpetual meddling with the affairs of Eastern Europe, and left them to Germany and Russia, the Great Powers immediately concerned. Strategic thinking of this nature was quite beyond the scope of politicians and civil servants, embedded in the dust of ages. Judmas was also of their persuasion.

Such was the situation in 1937. A Germany stronger and more united than ever before in her history: France on the decline and ready to come to terms with her powerful neighbour—the only sane policy: Britain, who had missed the golden opportunity of settling with Germany whilst she was still weak, determined to thwart her in every direction now that she was strong.

Picture the reverse situation with Germany and Britain in alliance. The peace of the world would have been assured, and the countries of Europe would have been able to settle down, with Germany taking the lead in the direction and control of European economy. This was too much to expect of our hidebound leaders, but—oh, the pity of it!

XXVII.

However politics were not my business. I could only try and point out to my countrymen the strategic danger they were running so needlessly, by pursuit of a faulty foreign policy. I lectured in many parts of the country on this subject, and seldom refused an invitation, because I felt it was my duty to open as many people's eyes as possible, before the trouble began. I am going to mention one lecture in particular, and to give a few quotations from my own address, as well as some of the comments by the audience.

This lecture was delivered on the 1st February, 1938 at Chatham House, with the late Lieutenant-General Sir George Macdonogh in the Chair.

When I had been invited to speak, I mentioned that my views on the "Strategic Aspects of the Situation in the Far East" were hardly such as would appeal to members of the British Institute for International Affairs, who were carefully nurtured, as far as I knew, on sound League of Nations' principles. However, I was told that they liked to hear all sides of the subject, so the address was given.

At a later date, when I was safely locked up in Brixton Prison, a friend of mine who had attended the lecture, and remembered the clear warning I had given, went to Chatham House to try and get a copy of the proceedings, with the kind idea of letting some influential people know the type of person it was deemed necessary to keep behind bars. He was informed that the Council had directed that no record of the evening's entertainment was to be kept, a departure from the customary practice of the Institute. I was not surprised. Like the Biblical kings of old, these people only wanted to hear the prophets who prophesied favourably to their conceptions.

One of the members of the Council who was present was Mr. A. V. Alexander, the 'Co-op' king, who was later to abandon shops for ships as First Lord of the Admiralty. He cannot complain that he was not warned.

Fortunately I had retained my copy of the verbatim proceedings sent to me, presumably, by an oversight, so I am enabled to quote some of the remarks.

EXTRACTS FROM LECTURER'S REMARKS
"Now if you ask me which of the nations it is most important for us to be at peace with strategically, I should say Germany, Italy, and Japan: Germany for security in Home Waters, Italy for safety on our lines of communication to the Far East, and Japan to look after our interests

in the Far East. So that you see as far as strategy is concerned our foreign policy since the war has been disastrous. There are those three Powers with whom we should be on friendly terms, but who have been driven together by force of circumstances, and appear to have achieved a degree of Collective Security which has eluded its sponsors at Geneva.

"I do not suppose there has ever been a time in our history when it was more necessary for policy and strategy to go hand in hand; to be in double harness; and there has never been a time like recent years when they have been so estranged. Policy has kicked over the traces and has gone rushing ahead flogged by the pens and tongues of the idealists and intellectuals, whilst strategy has been lagging further and further astern maimed by the same instruments."

* * * *

"I do not know if you remember the situation at the beginning of the Great War. The War Office had made all their plans to send out the six divisions of the Expeditionary Force. The first three or four days of the war the Government debated whether they should send four divisions; should they send five divisions: should they send six divisions? Because of the danger of invasion. I might say that the danger of invasion was precisely nil from start to finish, but today they would be taking a very great risk if they sent out the whole fleet to the Far East. Every pen in Whitehall would be raising objections to this procedure. After all Security like Charity begins at home, so what I can see happening would be an entirely insufficient fleet rather like that which poor Rojdestvensky took out in the Russo-Japanese War, making the journey out to the Far East insufficiently equipped for its task. And then do not forget that Naval forces alone cannot bring a victory. They cannot bring sufficient pressure to bear to win a war. The Sea of Japan would probably be an impossible proposition, and the Japanese would be able to keep their communications open there with the mainland."

* * * *

"The Japanese found themselves in an impregnable position (*i.e.* after the Washington Naval Conference) and shortly afterwards they proceeded to explore it. This policy of Japan was nothing new. The "Times" correspondent, Dr. Morrison, who was out in Pekin some years before the war foretold the course which Japanese policy has taken, first in the venture in Korea, then in Manchuria, and then in China proper, where they intended to form a huge Eastern Empire which would meet the Western world in the middle of Asia. Dr. Morrison always contended, if that is any comfort, that the idea of the Japanese going to Australia was a bogey."

* * * *

"In conclusion I hope you will not think from my remarks tonight that I would stand for anything without retaliation because that is not my meaning at all. I have only tried to point out the folly of threatening when you cannot perform. There is no sentiment in politics and bluff is no good either, especially with dictators. If we are going to steer a safe course in the future between the many rocks and shoals ahead of us, then it is necessary for policy and strategy to be like a pair of Siamese twins, close together, side by side, otherwise we shall only suffer more humiliations like we did during the Abyssinian crisis, Manchukuo and so forth."

* * * *

FIELD MARSHAL SIR PHILIP CHETWODE* said that he had nothing to add, except that he would like to say as senior soldier there that he absolutely agreed with every word the lecturer had uttered. He had at first feared that when the lecturer had mentioned the Societies who talked about war so much, he would leave out the Archbishops. But he had not done so.

They had insisted upon holding a meeting in the Albert Hall, and talking the most frightful nonsense, in spite of the Christian Archbishop of Tokyo sending a telegram imploring them not to do so. The Archbishops and old women who knew nothing about the strategical aspects of the situation should realise that such talk, unless they were prepared to follow it up, did far more harm than good.

* * * *

---

* Now Lord Chetwode.

LORD STRABOLGI said that after the complete agreement of the eminent admiral and general he would like to add a little opposition.

The distinguished admiral and general who had just spoken were one hundred percent. pacifists.

If the type of fatalism shewn by a section of the Governing classes were to be allowed to spread, if everyone who stood up for British rights was to be called an old woman or a Red, if everyone knew that in no circumstances would Great Britain resist, of course every vestige of influence all over Asia, where prestige counted for so much, would go, and Britain's material possessions at the same time. For instance in Hong Kong there were several hundred thousand Chinese who were British subjects, who had built up their businesses as loyal subjects of the Crown. They would be betrayed.

It was true that Great Britain was weak. She was weak because she had failed in 1932 when America had been with her, when the sanctions policy had not been muddled over Italy, when the League had still been strong, when the Italian Navy had been very weak, when the German Navy had been practically non-existent, when the Japanese had had a strong peace party in their own country.

The speaker considered that a battleship base at Singapore had been a blunder. It was too far away with regard to Japan. Singapore was right on the equator, unsuitable for White men to live.

*   *   *   *

MAJOR NEAL said that having just come back from three very happy and healthy years in Singapore, he had had difficulty in remaining in his seat and hearing that Singapore was a place not fit for white men to live in.

*   *   *   *

ADMIRAL SIR HOWARD KELLY said that the reason Great Britain was forced to pursue this pacifist policy so plainly against her interests, was because of the work done by the Government to which the second speaker (Lord Strabolgi) had belonged, which had reduced the British Forces to such a state that not only could she not make war on anybody, but had been practically reduced to a situation where she was not able to keep the peace with anybody either.

Another point was the fairy tale of 1932. It would be interesting to know the origin of such a fairy tale. It bore no semblance of truth. At the time the speaker had been in command in China in 1931 and 1932. He had never seen any American help, on the contrary they had left him in the lurch every time. They had had no intention of taking action against the Japanese or against anybody, but had retired leaving the British in the lurch. The American Officer in command had told him to go ahead and do what he liked as he, the former, was not allowed to do anything at all, except give help and co-operation which he had done.

* * * *

THE RT. HON. A. V. ALEXANDER said that he had been amazed at the comments of the lecturer and of the late Commander-in-Chief in China who had last spoken. With regard to naval strengths and the share in reduction of naval strength which the second speaker (Lord Strabolgi) and his Government had had: the Government in question had only been in office two and a third years out of all the years since 1918. He himself had been, perhaps, more responsible than any other single person for the Treaty, not referred to by the lecturer, of 1930, passed when the lecturer had been one of his own staff at the Admiralty, and which had been considered by Lord Monsell and recently Winston Churchill, who had opposed it at the time, to have established a better relative naval security on a lower basis of naval units than even in 1914 and every naval authority with whom the speaker had consulted considered the replacement programme for cruisers established in 1930 had saved the British fleet in the cruiser section from rusting out from the bottom.

There was not a single naval authority today who would not agree that had it not been for the Labour Treaty of 1930 and the replacement programme during the period of financial depression there would not be a renewal of the cruiser fleet. The speaker had expected to hear from the lecturer who had been his intelligence officer at the Admiralty, a real instruction on strategy in the Far East.

What he had discovered to his horror was that the lecturer was of the school of thought who considered that if Great Britain could only drift long enough in her international relationships she would then be able, having withdrawn for so long on the territory of the whole Globe, to defend herself and the British Empire, if need be unilaterally against any comer at any point of the Commonwealth. Some of the wicked politicians ought to study strategy in the interests of the professional soldiers, sailors and airmen. The speaker believed from his reading and from advice from naval and military advisers that to defend the British Empire without powerful allies was an impossible strategical feat, and anyone who had made a real study of the post-war situation would agree that the soundest security for the British Commonwealth above any other interest was a real support at every right moment of the principle of Collective Security, binding signatures and the integrity of treaties.

* * * *

I have given these brief extracts from my Chatham House Lecture and its critics because they give a good idea of the muddled thought which was in vogue amongst the politicians during these critical years.

They were ready to fight anyone, anywhere, at any time in accordance with their new theories of international solidarity, and irrespective of strategical conditions. They had completely thrown overboard the sound principles upon which our Empire had been built up and successfully defended, and were prepared to waste our strength in military expeditions on the continent or elsewhere, which we had always avoided in the past. Mr. Alexander, a grocer at sea, was full of the necessity of co-operation as befitted an expert on Co-operative Societies, upon whose territory I should not dream of trespassing, because I do not know anything about the subject.

He avoided entirely my main criticism which was that we had allowed all the most valuable co-operators from a strategic point of view, to escape into the opposite camp, but I will not enlarge upon this matter here, because I hope I have made it plain already.

The 1930 Treaty on cruisers which he evidently regarded as a feather in his cap was a naval disadvantage which we had side-tracked successfully at Washington in 1922, because we were most anxious not to have our cruiser needs the subject of any international agreement, in view of our world-wide commitments, which are so much greater than those of any other nation. Mr. Alexander's remarks on this subject were just political clap-trap.

I had never suggested that the wicked politicians should study strategy, because I doubt if they would be any the wiser if they did, and the amateur strategist is a holy terror.

We gave up the Anglo-Japanese Alliance of our own accord: we quarrelled with Italy clumsily and unnecessarily: and now we were adding Germany to our list of adversaries. I cannot believe that any naval strategist born outside a lunatic asylum could have told Mr. Alexander that this was a healthy combination for our Empire to face at its present stage of development, or that the Collective Security upon which he and his friends were counting, could be regarded as a satisfactory remedy.

The politicians were not prepared to revise their political outlook to satisfy strategical requirements, and that is my grievance with them. Judmas cares nought for strategy and geopolitics, and our politicians were busy playing their international game without reference to the rules of sound strategy.

Lord Strabolgi's remarks were more from the soap-box orator's répertoire than from any other category, and a pretty ignorant one at that: witness his views on Hong Kong and Singapore.

It was hard to be called a pacifist by this windy demagogue. Had I been unkind, I should have whispered the mystic word "Bullfinch" which always has a chastening effect on him. Don't ask me why: ask him. When I was at Brixton, and possibly feeling less mellow, one of the prison officers told me that he was attending a lecture by Lord Strabolgi, so I gave him the password, which he informed me subsequently he had used with great effect.

Sir Howard Kelly's mystification in regard to the fairy tale of American help in 1932, only shows that he is not acquainted with Judmas and its ramifications, or the fairy tale would have become a commonplace.

I can only regret that events fully justified my warning, and that, amongst other things, Admiral Tom Phillipps and his meagre cortège were sacrificed to the political need of shewing that the Government were trying to do something to conceal their ineptitude.

With reference to Sir Philip Chetwode's remarks on the Bishops, nobody regrets more than I do that I found it necessary to attack them, but it is their own doing.

If they would only remain on their pedestals and confine their attention to ecclesiastical matters, I should not dream of commenting upon their activities, except in a spirit of reverence. But when they unship their halos and descend into the dust and strife of the market-place, in order to discuss foreign policy in connection with strategy, upon which they are ill-informed, they lay themselves open to most undesirable comments from rude persons like myself.

We pay our Bishops to shew us how to gain Heaven, not how to lose Singapore.

Upon another occasion I gave an address to the Royal Empire Society, with the late Admiral of the Fleet Lord Jellicoe in the chair, a man loved and respected throughout the navy and the country at large. He made some very kind remarks about myself, and said that he wished some of the people in 'high positions' had been present to hear what I had to say.

I presume that he was referring to the queer specimens, financial wizards, business men and Jews who were running and ruining the country.

The genuine 'highest in the land,' the men of lofty principle and integrity, who had presided over our destinies during the period of our real greatness, had been elbowed out long ago by the new plutocrats.

Being wise after the event, I think it was just as well that 'the people in high positions' were not present, or I might have paid an even longer visit to Brixton gaol, as a guest of these very gentlemen.

XXVIII.

Now we have reached the time, September, 1937, when I and several friends who held similar views, felt that an urgent need existed for the establishment of an Association to foster the mutual knowledge and understanding that ought to exist between the British and German peoples, and to counteract the flood of lies with which our people were being regaled in their daily papers. We all know that Truth is the first casualty in time of war, but on this occasion the poor lady was defunct long before war started. With these worthy objects in view, we founded the 'Link,' the Anglo-German organisation which helped to bring me safely to anchor in Brixton prison, after a brief and stormy voyage.

Our problem was not easy. Obviously we had to keep clear of any political activities, or we should find ourselves in trouble at once, with the world in such an inflammable condition. If we did not fall foul of the Scylla of our own Government, we should founder on the Charybdis of the Nazi régime.

So we limited our activities to non-political matters.

There was in existence already an Anglo-German Fellowship, of which I was a member of the Council. I was never very happy about this Association, which catered mainly for the well-to-do, and was largely supported by big business firms, interested in clearing the ground for an extension of commercial relations. It was also well patronised by Judmas, and its offshoots in British social and business circles.

In the event, the Fellowship closed down when the political situation got very strained in the Spring of 1939, thus giving an indication that its cause was regarded as hopeless, and adding its small influence to the generally deteriorating atmosphere of European affairs.

Mr. C. E. Carroll, Editor of the Anglo-German Review, was the first person to suggest the foundation of the 'Link.' Badly wounded in the Great War in 1916, he became an Air Force pilot on recovery, although suffering a fifty percent disability from his wounds. He was shot down over Belgium and captured by the Germans, on this occasion only slightly wounded. He escaped and eventually reached England just before the Armistice. A born journalist, he edited the British Legion paper for some time, and then started the Anglo-German Review, so firmly was he imbued with the urgent need for furthering a better understanding between the two countries. He worked unsparingly at this excellent little monthly thinking nothing of toiling for several successive nights, until the midnight oil was replaced by the light of day.

Always under-staffed and short of funds, he did most of the office work himself, and no individual could have done more to attempt to stop the approaching tragedy.

He found a snug berth waiting for him in Brixton Prison as a grateful country's reward for his valuable services. He found out, too, what it meant to incur the displeasure of Judmas.

Membership of the 'L i n k' was open to all; to anyone with enough sense to realise that the establishment of good relations between English and German people was the best work to which any man and woman could apply themselves, if they wished to avoid a cataclysm.

We opened branches gradually all over the country, including several in London and its suburbs. I spent a great deal of time travelling all over England and Scotland, to address members of new Branches; I never got as far as Ireland, or to any of the Branches started by enthusiasts in the Dominions.

We found many ways of putting our members and Germans in touch, and arranged tours to Germany with a friendly welcome for the visitors on the other side: we also looked after many Germans coming to this country. My great regret is that we had not started a few years earlier, as we should have had time to collect an enormous membership, and the task of the war-mongers in this country would have been much harder.

As it was, we could hardly have started at a worse moment, as Herr Hitler began shortly afterwards to make things difficult for us, by the successive shocks he administered to a panicky Europe, when he began to incorporate into the Reich sundry outlying German communities, commencing with Austria in the Spring of 1938. This little country had been emasculated by the Peace Treaties, and left with a hopeless future, unless permitted to work in unison with the Reich.

Needless to say, we encountered much opposition from the many interests in this country, which were determined to quarrel with Hitler's new order in Europe.

The Jews and official Labour were the most bitter of our opponents, and lost no opportunity of trying to discredit our work. Jewish hatred of Germany was easier to understand than that of Labour, to those unacquainted with the machinations of Judmas. Threats, too, were not lacking, but we continued to make progress in spite of all hostility, although it was uphill work against the constant output of vituperation and falsehood, appearing in the columns of our inspired national Press. Those members who went to Germany, returned aghast at the misrepresentations of our Papers, and were the best recruiting sergeants we had. The Munich settlement in the autumn of 1938 was a setback to the war-mongers, but had a retarding effect on the 'Link's' progress as well, which was not surprising. Public opinion was completely bemused.

Today, a "Man of Munich" is used by our gutter Press as a term of contumely. I wonder what our descendants a hundred years hence will have to say about it. Whatever their verdict, which largely depends on the nature of the 'historians,' I only desire that my name be written humbly on the scroll of the "Men of Munich," in other words that I may be counted as one of the men who remained free from the seductions of those aliens who were trying to get us to fight their battles for them, instead of putting British interests first.

It must always be remembered that no "Men of Munich" would have been needed, if the statesmen of Europe had been sincere in their desire for peace, as no Munich crisis would have been reached. The matters crying out for settlement in Europe would have been brought to the Council table at a much earlier date.

But Judmas had no intention of allowing such a happy solution to be achieved, and its political henchmen made no serious efforts in this direction.

After all, excuses for future wars must be left ready to hand, so as to conceal the real motives.

XXIX.

In the spring of 1939 Mr. Chamberlain's Government gave the guarantee to Poland which brought war very much closer, indeed, made it almost a certainty.

Great pressure must have been brought to bear on Mr. Chamberlain to give his consent to this extraordinary declaration, by which we engaged ourselves to ensure the security and integrity of a country, to which we could in no manner bring any direct form of military support.

In effect, we were saying to Poland "If you are prepared to withstand the German demands, however reasonable, and are ready to accept the consequences in the shape of the extinction of your country by defeat in war, then we will guarantee that you shall be restored to your former condition at the end of hostilities."

We do not know to what extent the Poles were alive to the full implication of this dud cheque, which, on the face of it, is one of the most cynical and disreputable actions ever taken by a British Government. The most charitable view to take is that they thought it would frighten the Germans out of their contemplated action, because that makes them merely ignorant, and not downright dishonest. Mr. Buchanan, who left Gdynia just before the outbreak of war, said in the House on the 30th October, 1939, that Poland would never have gone to war, if its inhabitants had realised how they were going to be left in the lurch by England. I am tired of reading in the Press that our national honour demanded that this guarantee should be given, and similar unctuous sentiments. What nauseous hypocrisy: what an abuse of the meaning of words. No guarantee incapable of fulfilment can be termed a matter of national honour by any possible interpretation: dishonour would be nearer the mark.

Another comforting theory frequently advanced in the papers is that the same standard of honour cannot be expected in international dealings, as exists between men of good faith in their personal relations. If that were true, no wonder we have got into such a muddle, and general atmosphere of distrust.

As long as Judmas is pulling the strings, I agree cordially that honesty need not be expected, but until nations can trust one another's word, a feeling of tension will persist, and no lasting peace can be anticipated.

Mutual trust cannot result until the word of a statesman means what the dictionary intended it should mean.

Today we look round the world at numerous scrap-heaps of broken pledges and treaties.

The theory of a sliding scale in terms of honour may prove a very soothing anodyne to the consciences of those engaged in that pleasant game of double-crossing known as diplomacy, but let us hope we shall live to see the days when we can say once more that an Englishman's word is his bond. I am glad that I have not got the pledge to Poland on my conscience.

The Poles are a brave, arrogant and self-confident race, needing the curb rather than the spur: any encouragement they may have derived from our guarantee was an incentive to opposition to their powerful neighbour's demands. For what was the simple logic of the whole matter? Poland redivivus was a small country sandwiched between two powerful neighbours—Germany and Soviet Russia. Poland could only hope to maintain a prosperous existence by keeping on good terms with both of them. This was not possible so long as she remained in possession of stolen property, the legacy of the Peace Treaties.

Even at that time of post-war delirium, the wiser heads, Smuts and Lloyd George amongst them, realised that the Poland established by the fatuous Treaty to which they had appended their signatures, was the most fruitful breeding-ground in Europe for the germs of future wars. The French were mainly responsible for the arrangement, which was a part of their encircling policy towards Germany. They trained the Polish army, which felt itself ready for all comers.

The Poles had always shewn an incapacity for good government in the past: in the twenty years that had elapsed since the Great War they had maintained this reputation, although it is only fair to say that they were terribly handicapped by post-war conditions in a land which had experienced the full blast of the tempest. Whilst this might condone the low standard of living amongst the population, approximating in many parts to that of the beasts of the field, it did not excuse their highly injudicious treatment of their minorities, whom they should have gone out of their way to conciliate, if they aspired to any permanent future.

All said and done, the unpleasant feeling persists that we were not thinking so much of the Poles when we gave the guarantee, as of 'daring' Hitler, by erecting a starting-gate for the next European War, of which he could not possibly plead ignorance. If we were so bent on opposing Hitler's European projects, we should have chosen a starting-gate up to which we could, at any rate, have flogged our war-horse.

But it is of no use giving your jockey his riding instructions for Newmarket, if the race is to take place in Warsaw, time and date unknown. Of course the answer is that we wanted our horse entered for the next race-meeting, wherever it took place, and we strongly suspected that it would be held at Warsaw.

This was just too bad for the Poles, but after all, they could cancel the meeting if they so wanted, in spite of the promising entry, which tempted them to persist.

If only Mr. Neville Chamberlain had continued to follow his own sensible policy, and had appealed to the country for a mandate instead, before giving the guarantee, he would have shown himself to be a great man, who was not going to be led away from his country's true interests by the petty considerations of party politics, or by the taunts and howlings of the jackals of Fleet Street.

If he had failed to carry his views, he would still have left a great name behind him in the pages of history, written by unbiased British pens in the future. As it was, he allowed himself to be swept along in the current of popular sentiment, largely whipped up by Judmas, and his name is now held up to opprobrium by those evil men who were determined to thwart his sound instincts, which he had not got the courage to follow in the day of trial. He will remain to me always as a good man, who knew what was right, but who had not got the strength of character to back his convictions to the bitter end. Yet on the degree of courage and determination shewn by this provincial mayor depended the whole future of our Empire.

XXX.

Things got more and more difficult for the 'Link' as 1939 rolled along, and international tension increased.

We never gave up hope, and felt that we ought to persevere right up to the last possible moment, as any relaxation of our activities would only look as if we regarded the patient as beyond further human aid. The Anglo-German Fellowship passed out of business as I have already related, and that made it all the more necessary for us to keep one lifebuoy on the stormy waters of Anglo-German relations.

The egregious Mander and others of a similar kidney, were sniping at us in the House of Commons, and the Jews were attacking us from every possible angle.

In vain we pleaded that we had never attacked the Jews, and that the 'Link' was anti-nobody in its policy. The very fact that we advocated a friendly understanding between the British and German peoples was counted as an anti-Jewish activity in Jewish mentality. In other words if one was dubbed 'pro-German,' one became automatically 'anti-Semitic,' a curious anomaly, but any stick was good enough to beat the people who were opposing the war, as being contrary to British interests.

I was qualifying rapidly as an opsimath in Jewish matters. To give an example of Press malevolence, one of the worst of the weekly rags published a row of ghastly looking heads, representing myself and other members of the 'Link' Council, over the caption 'And the Jews.'

I was portrayed with any hair Providence has left me in wild confusion, mouth agape, and apparently declaiming in the best Hyde Park tradition. This puzzled me considerably.

I had no delusions about my facial attractions, but I knew that I had never looked like that when addressing a meeting.

A closer inspection revealed an unmistakable landmark—the gaudy tie of the Admiralty Golfing Society.

Memory functioned. About ten years previously, I had made one of my rare appearances in a Golf match against the Press at Walton Heath, at which photographs were taken. I am a bad golfer: it was a windy day. Evidently I had just made a stroke which was unsuccessful in keeping the ball in the straight and narrow way. I was gazing open-mouthed at my failure; thus the camera caught me, and the result was saved for future use, in case I offended Fleet Street at any time. I sent to the Agency concerned, and procured a copy of the identical photograph. There is no trick too mean for Judmas to employ against those who oppose their policy.

XXXI.

I had been trying for some time to start the corresponding 'L i n k' in Germany, and to put branches with similar interests in the two countries, in touch with one another, so that they could visit and correspond. I was very keen on this idea.

At last we got the scheme to work, although the Germans preferred to call their organization the 'Ring;' I think their reason was that 'L i n k' was too much like 'links'—or left—conjuring up thoughts of Bolshevism and Jews, and all the other Nazi taboos. In this manner Bath and Salzburg were associated, as both places could claim musical affinities.

I arranged to go out to Salzburg with about a hundred other 'L i n k' members, mostly from the Bath branch, to assist at the inauguration of the first Branch of the 'Ring' to take shape. I went by air to Munich at the end of July, 1939. Here I joined the rest of the party, most of whom had preceded me by train. We had a delightful drive to Salzburg, in charge of our hospitable hosts. A few of us were accommodated at the Schloss Leopolds-

Kron, the lovely old Palace of the Archbishops, which had been kindly placed at our disposal.

I was looking forward to a very happy week of festivities, but unfortunately, taking advantage of my absence abroad, a vicious attack was launched upon the 'Link' in the House of Commons.

My visit was completely spoiled by repeated calls to the telephone, mostly from an excited Press, on the track of a very toothsome morsel, from the Judmas point of view.

The reply in the House which had raised such a commotion was made by the Home Secretary, who was none other than our old friend Slippery Sam Hoare, whom we last saw weeping on the Front Bench over the Abyssinian fiasco.

He had only had to remain a very short time "*en disponibilité*"; political gems, cut by international experts are rare; so here he was, back in the Troupe again, but playing a new part.

General Post is one of the most popular games amongst our leading politicians: I have not played it myself since nursery days, but it must be much more exciting as played under Westminster Rules. A really good player has only to make a sufficient mess of one job, to be able to pass on to a fresh thrill, leaving behind a trail of mischief, to be cleared up by some other poor devil.

The Post goes from—Oh, I must take a hand at this fascinating game. Perhaps I can stand as an Independent 18B candidate at the next General Election.

Possibly some of the Old Firm will have been prised out of their seats by that time: I sincerely hope so, for their country's sake. However, to return to Sam, he thought he was batting on a good wicket this time, smirching the reputations of his countrymen, with many admirers to hand him a bouquet.

The burden of his accusation against the 'Link' was that it was German-controlled and German-paid, a pair of thumping lies that left that poor old tax-dodger Ananias toiling far in the rear. Nowadays politicians do not mind being told that they have lied: I suppose they get so used to it.

This is one of the most deplorable features of latter-day democracy. It appears to be quite in order for a Minister of the Crown to stand up in his place and utter the most barefaced falsehoods without loss of prestige, provided of course, he lies in the right direction—fully approved by the powers that be.

Nobody seems to mind that the standard of honesty has fallen so low. It is a bad sign.

Take the case of Hore Belisha, a Minister who should have been above reproach.

One fine day he loses his job, and the next he is subjected to the most devastating exposure in Truth that I ever remembered reading. If all the allegations were true, the man was a most unfortunate financier, to put it mildly.

What does he do? Invoke the law to clear his name? Not a bit of it. I can only presume that he dare not do so.

The sole visible, or invisible, effect, was that copies of "Truth" in club smoking-rooms disappeared, or were found with a page missing. But all the members of the House got a copy. What did they do? Nothing. He had not transgressed the law, so why worry? There are plenty more in similar case, and there he sits today. It amazes me, who was brought up to very different standards.

Then Mr. Boothby—well, he was unlucky—he received a slight reproof from his parliamentary leader, but he still sits there. He took a temporary interest in 18B; one of his friends, Mr. Richard Weiniger, the money-spinner, had got caught in the toils. It appeared as if a mistake had been made in this case as he was quickly released.

Since Big Business invaded the House in force, the standard of integrity has seriously deteriorated. The temptation to combine business with politics proves too strong.

XXXII.

The statements made by Sir Samuel Hoare about the 'Link' at a time when the public were being educated to war by every possible means, were hailed with delight by a hungry Press, who like nothing better than to introduce a few personalities into their campaign of hatred. And to find an admiral at the head of this wicked conspiracy —well, it was just too wonderful.

When I landed at Croydon a few nights later, I found an eager ring armed with note-books and cameras, in spite of the lateness of the hour. Time is nothing to Fleet Street, if only the muck-raking is good.

An official 'Link' reply to Sir Samuel Hoare's strictures had been postponed until my return. We held a Council meeting to which the Press were admitted, and issued subsequently the following communication, which, needless to say, few papers had the honesty or decency to publish in full:—

"The 'Link' Council consider that if the Secretary of State for Home Affairs had reason to suspect the character and purpose of the 'Link,' he should have approached them with a view to obtaining full information regarding their activities. Instead, Sir Samuel Hoare resorted to methods which the Council strongly deprecate as being inaccurate and unreliable. Questions have frequently been asked in the House of Commons about the Link: such observations are privileged.

"On one such occasion Admiral Sir Barry Domvile, Chairman of the 'Link,' wrote to Sir Samuel Hoare and invited him to make a thorough investigation, offering to place at his disposal all the relative papers and documents. This proposal was ignored. Sir Samuel Hoare's statement in reply to a question of Mr. Mander's in the House last Thursday is a travesty of the facts. The Council deny emphatically the truth of any of Sir Samuel's suggestions.

"Not a penny piece has come from abroad to support the 'Link' funds. It is true that Sir Samuel only made this suggestion by innuendo, but that was sufficient warrant, coming from a responsible official, for the Press to base a charge of 'Nazi-money' having been received by the 'Link.'

"The assertion that the 'Link' is an instrument of the German Propaganda Ministry is equally absurd. How can a Council controlling its own policy and handling its own affairs be anybody's instrument?

"The 'Link's' creed is simple: the members believe that mutual sympathy and understanding between the peoples of Great Britain and Germany are essential to any stability in the world: to this end they work in many directions, all non-political. For example tours, exchanges, and pen correspondents are arranged, and many Germans are entertained in this country.

"If the Government desire that no efforts be made to establish these friendly feelings and relations between two great nations, they must say so, and the 'Link's' activities will temporarily cease, as behoves loyal citizens.

"If, on the other hand—and the Council find it difficult to believe that this is not so—the Government do not wish to restrain the efforts of private individuals in this direction, the Council hope that this constant sniping at their activities from official quarters will cease, and that they will be permitted to continue their work without unnecessary opposition."

Rather a poser for Sam, who wisely took no notice of it: denigration is so much easier than justification—and more Sam-worthy.

Why did not the man call me out any way, for telling him he was a liar? That is not a privileged statement, and I should like to have taken a shot at him on Putney Heath: perhaps he was afraid of blubbing in the middle, and offering me a sitter. I will keep the invitation open; any day, any hour, provided he does not make it too late in the afternoon for me to go down afterwards and order a wreath at the Putney florist's, before going home for tea.

I also issued a message to 'Link' members from which the following is an extract. It reads sadly today:—

"A few members resigned, but a very much larger number has joined. Many people felt that there must be something wrong when a Minister of the Crown used his privileged position in the House of Commons, to belittle the activities of people who are taking no lessons in patriotism from him or anyone else.

"That the 'Link' is pro-British to the core goes without saying. Its members advocate a close and friendly understanding with the German people, because they have the vision to realise that it is the only road to continued happiness and prosperity in their own Empire. Anglo-German friendship is the keystone to peace in the world."

I must admit that I was pleasantly surprised by the increase of membership referred to above. I was particularly glad to welcome the Duke of Westminster in this manner: a firm opponent of humbug and chicanery.

I only wish that he and his kind had played a more prominent part in public life in recent years: they might have made a lot of difference to the country's future.

It is significant that the Government never dared shut up any members of the House of Lords under their 18B ramp.

I think they knew that their Lordships, in spite of their clipped wings, would be much quicker to resent insults to their members than were the members of the Lower House, who saw with hardly a dissentient voice, one of their number, Captain Ramsay, shut up for years, because he had offended the hidden powers.

I wonder what the stalwarts of the past must have thought when they looked down on their spineless successors, with their misplaced humility.

This surrender of their age-long rights with barely a murmur is an ominous sign of the paralysis which overtakes those who allow themselves to be made the tools of others.

XXXIII.

Whilst at Salzburg, I had been very careful to keep clear of official Nazidom, because I did not want to give the slightest excuse for an accusation of meddling in affairs which were not my concern.

However Herr Walther Hewel turned up one afternoon to see me at the Schloss, and as his remarks are of a little interest, I place them on record.

Hewel was a young man who had been at Hitler's side during the Munich Putsch, and had shielded him from injury with his own body when the firing began. He was now Hitler's constant companion; a stolid, dependable type of person, probably soothing to a man of Hitler's temperament: not overgifted with brains, I should imagine, but full of sound commonsense.

He appeared to be rather nervous and ill-at-ease, and began by asking whether England was going to fight.

I replied that I knew no more than what I read in the papers: he was aware that I always kept clear of officialdom: I was quite certain that if Germany attacked Poland, we should fulfil our guarantee to that country.

He responded that he had never seen Hitler so composed and certain of himself: that the impending struggle was a catastrophe which could easily have been avoided, if only the statesmen of Europe had realised that Hitler was a great man, and not just a charlatan. (A curious word to use). They had appeared to think that Hitler and his régime would not last long, and that all his offers of a reduction in armaments, and similar peaceable proposals, could be safely ignored, as he would not remain long enough in a position to ensure that they would be carried out by Germany. He said that the war would only be a war of prestige for us.

So we parted with sorrow in our hearts that events appeared to be hastening to the inevitable climax, and that the two great countries which could have led the rest of the world to a peaceful settlement of outstanding problems, would be shortly engaged in deadly combat, from which others, less worthy, would probably extract the pickings.

The poison of deadly hatred against Germany was already too deeply injected in British veins by the Judmas hypodermic syringe, for any alternative to be possible. We were approaching one of the saddest and most fateful moments in the history of the world.

XXXIV.

At about the same time as the events just recorded, our Government had been struck by the bright idea that it would not be a bad plan to have an ally on soil adjoining Polish territory—in fact that it was essential, if the guarantee was to be worth the paper upon which it was written.

So we embarked upon one of the most humiliating set of negotiations in our history: futile from the start, and in which our delegates were treated with a gross lack of courtesy.

Stalin's one idea was to see the rest of Europe happily at war, so that on its conclusion he could step in, fresh and vigorous, and paint the whole lot red: a risky game, but one that had been played successfully before.

His immediate aim must be, therefore, to start the ball rolling. This could only be accomplished by quieting German fears of an attack on both flanks, their historical prepossession, which might have made Hitler pause before his assault on Poland.

Stalin welcomed our overtures, as they enabled him to put the screw on Hitler, and thus obtain better terms over the non-aggression pact which he was busily negotiating, in the shape of a fatter cut off the Polish joint.

We played the Russian game admirably, and sent our admiral and his staff of experts to Moscow, to be led up the garden path. Thus Hitler and Stalin were enabled to come to terms over one of the most immoral pacts in history, which neither of them could have believed would last long, although it suited their purpose at the time. We were made to look foolish, when the world saw how we had been double-crossed by the wily Georgian.

In view of subsequent events, it is open to wonder whether either or both of the successful pact-makers ever regretted their infamous achievement.

XXXV.

The last number of the Anglo-German Review, the organ of publicity used by the 'Link,' appeared a few days before the 3rd September, 1939, the day which brought the 'Link's' brief career to an automatic close, which will, I hope, only be temporary.

This final number contained an illustrated account of our trip to Salzburg, together with information regarding our fracas with the Government.

I shall always treasure my copy, which recalls the failure of a vain hope, but leaves me happy in my mind, as I feel I could not have done more as a private individual, to try and stave off the impending calamity, the greatest betrayal of the British people in the whole of their history.

The first duty of any form of Government is to promote the welfare of its own subjects, and not to sacrifice their lives uselessly, in an endeavour to exercise parental control over a reluctant world, mainly at the behest of a powerful alien minority.

XXXVI.

The early months of the war passed quietly, except for the wretched Poles. The Government's impressions of the probable reactions of the German people to war, were hopelessly at fault. At least, that is the only possible explanation of the absurd crop of leaflets, which were broadcast over German soil, shortly after we had declared war. The intense enthusiasm of the German people for the Nazi régime, and the hopes thereby engendered in German bosoms of achieving at last their rightful position in the world, were given little credence in this country. Too much attention must have been paid to the views of Judmas, and of the naturally biased refugees from the Reich.

To drop doctrinaire leaflets at this stage of the war was equivalent to an endeavour to appease a charging tiger with lumps of sugar: 'confetti' the Dutch called them.

So Poland suffered its lonely martyrdom, whilst England and France, its guarantors, watched in impotence.

The uncanny lull lasted through the first winter of the war. Early in 1940 a friend wrote to me that Neville Chamberlain had remarked that if he could arrange for a little fighting in the spring, he thought he would be ready for peace by the autumn. This sounded incredible; a child playing with the matches: just as if he was saying that the boys must not be disappointed now that they were all dressed up in their new and revolting clothes. Just a bit of summer fun, and then the olive branch. Dear! Dear!

Then the Nazi sluices were opened. Denmark, Norway, Luxemburg and the Low Countries were over-run by the German hordes.

Churchill became Prime Minister on the 10th May; poor Neville Chamberlain was swept away in a flood of recrimination. The new régime brought fresh policies in its train, and shortly afterwards we became its victims.

Before entering Brixton, however, it will assist this tale to make a brief survey of Judmas, that sinister agency which has wrought such harm to the interests of our great Empire.

XXXVII.

Judmas is my copyright title for the Judaeo-Masonic combination, which has been the principal disturbing factor in world politics for many a long day. There is nothing new about Judmas; for several centuries now, it has been behind most of the wars and revolutionary movements in Europe, and to some extent in other parts of the world.

It is a tragedy that the British people have been so ill-informed on this crucial matter, and so careless of the way in which they have been governed, as to permit this secret Junta to gain such control over their affairs.

This has not come about through lack of literature on the subject. There are books galore exposing the dangers to which the nations lie bare, as long as they leave these unconfined powers at work in secret behind the scenes.

These books date back over a very long period, but specially large numbers have been published in recent years. Many are written by Jews, who are fortunately given to boasting of their achievements and plans, or we should know less about them.

These books will not be found exposed to view in the library or bookshop, nor will any encouragement to read them be found in the Press or in book reviews. Judmas can take care of all these sources of information. It cannot prevent books from being published and read, by those who get to hear of them, although sometimes whole editions are bought up, to prevent circulation.

This is not a textbook on Judmas: here I cannot do more than touch briefly on the subject. Those who wish to know more must study for themselves, if they can get the books: then keep their eyes open, and put two and two together.

An elementary book on the subject is that of the Vicomte Léon de Poncins "The Secret Powers Behind Revolution," which was published in 1929 by the Boswell Publishing Company Limited of 10, Essex Street, Strand. This book is clear, moderate, up-to-date, and well documented, partly from Jewish sources, but is unfortunately out-of-print.

I knew nothing of the Jewish question until a few years ago, and had no special feelings in regard to Jews, amongst whom I had many friends. I hope that I shall still have some left, after what I have got to say. The activities of Judmas are confined to a small section of both Jews and Masons: the large majority have no idea of the work undertaken behind the façade of Judmas.

At the beginning of this tale I said that I had felt for many years that there was some hidden Power at work behind the Government, but that I had no means of discovering where this Power lay: nor had I much curiosity, only a vague uneasiness at something intangible and inexplicable.

This feeling was especially prevalent when dealing with the upper tiers of the Civil Service in the Government Offices.

Only in recent years have my eyes been opened to the mystery, and once this had happened, all the missing pieces fell into place like a jig-saw puzzle, except that I do not know to this day how many of the agents are aware of what they are doing, and I have a very high regard for officers of the Civil Service as a whole. I suppose that it was Hitler's attack on Judmas that really started me thinking, and my personal experience with the 'Link' that made me realise the strength of the forces arrayed against my humble efforts.

I do not blame the Jews, except so far as their aims are inhuman: they have a definite policy, and the skill and secrecy with which they conduct it, evoke my admiration. The organisation must be well nigh perfect, as it manages to keep its secrets so well hidden: only occasionally the veil is lifted.

The trouble is that this policy, so inexorably pursued, is not one that should commend itself to the Governments of nations who have the best interests of their peoples at heart.

For the aim of these international Jews is a World state kept in subjection by the power of money, and working for its Jewish masters. You may find this fantastic, but do not be too ready to laugh it away, or you will only be qualifying yourself for another British Ostrich of which there are too many in existence already. If some of us had been a little more wide awake in the past, the world might have been spared untold misery.

XXXVIII.

About twenty years ago, considerable excitement was caused by the publication in this country of a little book entitled "The Protocols of the Learned Elders of Zion." These protocols explained at length the objects of Bolshevism and the methods of attaining this earthly Paradise, the whole forming one of the most cruel and inhuman documents ever published.

This book was translated into English by Mr. Victor Marsden, formerly Russian Correspondent of "The Morning Post" and resident in Russia for many years. The material was extracted from a Russian book published by Professor Nilus in 1905, of which a copy exists, or existed, in the British Museum. Mr. Marsden considered that the Protocols were issued at the first Zionist Conference held at Basle in 1897.

Every effort was made to suppress Dr. Nilus's book after the 1917 revolution in Russia, all copies that could be found being impounded and destroyed.

There was a storm of indignation in the Jewish world when Mr. Marsden's work appeared, and the Protocols were denounced as forgeries, without any attempt being made to rebut their hideous theme.

Neither you nor I are in a position to know the truth of the matter. One thing can, however, be asserted with complete confidence: if the Protocols are a forgery, either the perpetrator was one of the most remarkable prophets the world has ever seen, or else he was so well acquainted with the aims of International Jewry, that he was able to present an accurate forecast of future developments.

Nobody can read the Protocols without being struck by their close resemblance to recent world happenings. When so much has been proved true already, or is in process of making world history today, it is a fairly safe bet to back the remainder to come off, if Judmas remains in control.

The connection between Jewry and Freemasonry is clearly set forth: in brief, Masonry is the executive partner for the conduct of Jewish policy.

The authorship of the Protocols becomes immaterial, once it has been established that they contain a genuine policy, now in process of development before our eyes.

In 1920, the "Times," which at that time still retained the highly respected influence of the Walter family, published an article entitled "The Jewish Peril," which included the following remarks:—

"No one can fail to recognise Soviet Russia in the Protocols, and no one can deny that the Commissars of the Soviets are nearly all Jews.

"Whence comes the uncanny note of prophecy, in part fulfilled, in part far gone in the way of fulfilment? Have we been struggling all these tragic years to blow up and extirpate the secret organisation of German world domination, only to find beneath it *another more dangerous* because *more secret?*
Have we by straining every fibre of our national body, escaped a 'Pax Germanica' only to fall into a 'Pax Judaica?' "

Under the same management today, the "Times" could have answered these ominous queries with a certainty —but no, I had forgotten 18B. The management and all the staff would have been snugly interned, and the paper would have been edited by a 'Frond' of Bracken, or some other more amenable journalist.

XXXIX.

The famous, or should I say, infamous, 18B Defence Regulation, under which many of us have been suffering, is clearly outlined in the Protocols. Curiously enough Protocol No. 18 is one of those involved.

Everything points to the fact that Jewry is closely connected with the conception and conduct of this Regulation.

Let me mention just a few indications of this nature, which came within my immediate purview:—

1. Two Jews, of whom I had no personal knowledge, asked in the House of Commons why I was at large: I wasn't for much longer. One of them, by name Strauss, became subsequently Morrison's parliamentary private secretary, where he could keep his eye on him.

2. A Jew called Abrahams came down to my home to assist the police with my arrest. He boasted about this to his friends, from one of whom I got the information: of course we had seen him at the time.

3. There were many Intelligence Officers of Jewish origin at the various internment camps for 18B prisoners.

4. Latchmere House, Ham Common, the third degree establishment of the British Ogpu was partially staffed by Jews.

I was not invited there myself, but my son spent a wretched month there, whilst his inquisitors were vainly endeavouring to find out what a wicked man his father was. I have had a look at the place, and its Commandant, since I came out.

5. The "Jewish Chronicle," which is the "Times" of Jewry, frequently contained a column headed in large type "Jewish Defence."

The contents of this column were nothing but the garbage the Editor could rake up in connection with 18B matters. It is reasonable to wonder what these doings, which the public were assured were concerned with national security, had in common with a column solely concerned with Jewish Defence.

6. I saw a letter from the Editor of the "Jewish Chronicle" to the wife of one of the 18B prisoners, expressing his perturbation at the nature of the releases which were taking place from the ranks of the 18B's, in which he could see no definite policy of any kind. Again, it is reasonable to ask what on earth the Editor of the "Jewish Chronicle" had to do with the policy of individual releases of persons suspected of being a danger to national security.

7. A neighbour of mine, who had been vainly trying to get employment, after a long term of imprisonment as an 18B, told me of his experience.

He had had a long and blameless record as a servant of the London Passenger Transport Board. Whenever he applied for a job, the Board informed his would-be employer of the unfortunate end to his service. On one such occasion he found a prosperous-looking Jew gazing at his record: he said "I cannot employ you, you don't like Jews." To which my poor comrade replied truthfully that he had no feelings against Jews. He was a Mason.

The only answer he got was "You must have, or you would not have been there."

It is inconceivable that all this Jewish connection with 18B affairs was purely accidental and disinterested. Everything points to the fact that Jewry was very intimately connected with the administration of the Regulation; in all probability, its main inspiration, so many things point this way.

The so-called Swinton Committee was closely concerned with 18B matters, and was consulted by Morrison before making releases.

Churchill refused to give the House any information about this Committee, but informed members that the Committee was directly responsible to him. So we knew that there was a Gentile in the Chair, but not that the Committee, from its general composition, might have been the Local Government Board of the Elders of Zion.

It looks very much as if 18B is a 20th Century edition of Shylock's pound of flesh: it may prove as ill-advised for its sponsors, as its prototype was to the Jew of Venice.

XL.

It was not necessary to have attacked the Jews to have incurred their enmity: merely to have attempted to thwart their policy in any direction was sufficient. And this is just what I had done in founding the 'Link.'

International Jewry was determined that nothing should stand in the way of war with Germany. I do not blame them for this, but am only engaged in shewing their power in the land, and their hold over their brother Gentiles.

We hear a great deal of the persecution of Jew by Gentile: in 18B we have the reverse process.

My whole-hearted contempt is reserved for those Gentiles who lent themselves to this policy, and without whose connivance, the persecution would not have been feasible.

We have reached a pretty pass in this country when such conduct of public affairs is possible.

Obviously the Jewish connection with 18B had to be concealed from the public, who, docile as they are, might have mustered a strong protest over such a scandalous happening.

This need for concealment lay at the root of all the secrecy maintained in the administration of the Regulation. The public had to be persuaded that the persons detained were suspected of hostile action, or contemplated action, against the State, whereas, in the main, they were those who had incurred the displeasure of Jewry.

The Jews had succeeded in establishing a state of affairs in which to be 'anti-Jewish' was equivalent to being 'pro-German.'

A certain number of 18B cases were deserving of suspicion, and gave a more genuine appearance to the unsavoury whole. All this is laid down in the Protocols.

I object to being dubbed anti-Jewish: I am not, but I am fully alive to the harmful activities of the most powerful section of Jewry, which are opposed to our national interests: I shall do my humble best to draw attention to the influence in our national policy exercised by these exotic Englishmen. That is the extent of my 'anti-Semitism.'

If our future were to remain indefinitely at the mercy of these alien interests, it would indeed be precarious.

Some people find it difficult to believe that the Jews are supporters of both Capitalism and Bolshevism. I do not know why these two policies should be incompatible: Bolshevism is nothing but State Capitalism. The truth is that the Jews, watching the social tendencies of the world, endeavour to cater for all tastes, only being concerned to maintain the whip hand. Capitalism and Bolshevism represent the upper and nether millstones of Jewish policy, between which the Gentiles can be ground into an amorphous mass, pliable to the handling of their masters.

Any counter-measures which it may be found necessary to adopt, in order to defeat these gentlemen, will press hardly on the many Jews who throw themselves heart and soul into the interests of their adopted countries, and soon become practically assimilated with the body of the nation, forming a valuable section of the community. It is unfortunate for them that their brethren whom we have been discussing, and who are engaged in furthering the aims of International Jewry, wish to have it both ways.

They desire to enjoy all the privileges and advantages to be found in the countries whose hospitality they are enjoying, and at the same time to remain free to further the plans of International Jewry, without reference to the advantages or disadvantages thereby entailed on their adopted lands. This is the main difficulty in dealing fairly with the Jewish problem.

The wide dispersal of Jewry throughout the world has enabled the international contingent to promote all sorts of plans for achieving their ends, which do not, or should not, commend themselves to the nations as a whole.

The various intensive national movements which we have been witnessing in recent years, are the revolt of the dissident nations against Jewish plans.

There is plenty of scope in the world for real co-operation amongst the nations, without trying to federate or amalgamate them, thus obliterating the national characteristics of which they are so rightly proud, not least the British people.

We have a special responsibility with our great Empire to set an example to the rest of the world, which they can copy if they like. It is not our business to try and force upon them a mode of living and design for Government, which may not suit their national tastes and habits, or the emergency of the day.

In this country in recent years, we have heard a great deal too much of internationalism, and all too little of our own task—the development and prosperity of our Empire on British lines.

Thanks to Churchill I nearly woke up a Frenchman one morning in 1940, and later on he tried to make me a Yankee. I have not got the slightest desire to be either, and I am quite sure neither France nor America wants me.

Surely in a democracy, the people should be consulted before any step pregnant with risks for their future, of this nature, is taken. Has Winston forgotten his Gilbert and Sullivan?

The neglect of our own Empire has been largely due to a mischievous desire to interfere all over the world.

If the example we set is good enough, others will follow it, but they do not want to be forcibly fed with Anglo-Saxon notions.

XLI.

I have not the least idea who the Elders of Zion may be, although I cannot help thinking that Mr. Israel Moses Sieff must be pretty high up in the hierarchy.

Unheard of in this country until after the last war, he appeared suddenly from nowhere, and began to work his way through the Money Power into a position of authority.

We come across his tracks everywhere: Marks and Spencer; the newspapers; house property; political and economic planning.

Mr. Sieff's photograph is not allowed to appear in the Press, and recently he visited the United States, and returned rather unexpectedly.

FROM ADMIRAL TO CABIN BOY 89

Now I see that his wife, Rebecca of that ilk, is running a campaign for the Women's Publicity Planning Association which aims at complete equality between the sexes, and is sponsoring a so-called Blanket Bill in the House of Commons, to sweep away all sex discrimination in one comprehensive motion.

So here we have Israel and Rebecca, strangers in the land, planning our lives for us. There must be something very wrong with England for such a situation to be possible.

Since when have we wanted this alien scheming for our future happiness? If I might hazard a guess, it would be that the Apostle Israel had come over to plumb the depths of the political situation in this once-contented little island, with a view to future policy. Otherwise I can make no sense of the sudden descent upon us of these two alien Jews to direct our affairs and tell us how to run our ancient land, with which they can have only a nodding acquaintance.

I suspect, too, that Judmas is in a hurry. Adolf Hitler upset the time-table by his direct challenge to its powers in Europe: this made war a certainty, if it could be brought about.

At the same time the long-term policy of Judmas had to be speeded-up, as too many people were getting wise to its activities. Judmas was at bay, and all the more dangerous and ruthless accordingly. Not lacking, however, in confidence.

In November, 1942, we find Mr. Greenwood telling a Jewish audience that the next twenty-five years would see their hopes fulfilled.

We are living in very queer times, and all good Englishmen should follow carefully the trend of events, or they may wake up one morning to find their birthright vanished.

XLII.

Freemasonry is the junior, but indispensable, partner in the Firm of Judmas. The large majority of Masons are blissfully ignorant, as far as I can make out, of the political uses to which their organisation is put, believing that its objects are confined to those proper to a mutual aid and benefit society.

The reasons why such secrecy is needed for this work, is not explained.

Examined from the viewpoint of Jewry, the need for the services of the junior partner is evident.

The Jews form only a small minority in each country, and would be unable to ensure the execution of their policy, unless they could obtain the collaboration of persons in the Government service. Obviously this could not be done openly, or the whole plan would be exposed and exploded.

They must therefore build up some secret organisation, and what could be better than the one already to hand, in which Jews figure so prominently?

That is the simple explanation, and it only became necessary to try and establish chosen men in key positions in the Government Offices, and in organisations like the police, to put the machine in working order.

It is impossible for an outsider to judge to what extent this policy is pursued; he can only watch results, and put two and two together.

The Protocols have a considerable bearing on the subject, and in my experience as an 18B, many remarkable corroborations were forthcoming.

I have often been told by Freemasons that British Masonry played no part in politics at all, and made a point of disassociating itself from the Continental organisations, which are openly political. This statement is quite untrue, and only goes to shew the ignorance that prevails in the lower ranks of Masonry.

It is only in the Government machine that Judmas has to plant its disciples in key positions.

Politicians, who come and go, need not necessarily be Masons. Their assistance can be procured by other and more direct means.

We all know that the Civil Service largely directs the policy of the country. The Press is never tired of telling us what an incomparable bureaucracy we possess: it is not difficult to guess whence the inspiration for these puffs comes.

I do not suggest for a moment that the men employed in furthering the aims of the Senior Partner are acting dishonestly. Many of them are firmly convinced that they are pursuing the country's best interests.

The fact remains, whether they know it or not, that the moving spirit is alien, and is concerned entirely with its own world-wide ambitions, and not with the prosperity of any individual land.

There are many people in this country today, who are so badly bitten by the International Bug, that they ignore completely the interests of their own land, in pursuit of a lot of half-baked international will-o'-the-wisps. These people fall easy victims to Judmas.

There is one subtle difference between the two partners in the Firm of Judmas. The members of the Junior branch—Liberals, Progressives, Planners, or whatever they call themselves, *think* that they are making use of International Jewry to further their aims for an earthly Elysium. On the other hand the Jews *know* that they are making use of the Planners to help them in establishing their dream of world domination.

When it comes to backing one's fancy, my money goes down on Jewry as a certain winner, in preference to any other candidate, to the last penny any of them leaves me.

XLIII.

Now for a word or two about my chief gaoler, Winston Churchill, and my more immediate turnkey, Herbert Morrison.

Churchill is one of the leading Jewish enthusiasts in the country, and the Jews are generally credited with having an undue influence in the creation of Governments. Possibly they entertained the belief that Mr. Churchill would be a suitable head-butler, provided he did not drop the tray too often, in which event he could, presumably, be ruthlessly dismissed. I do not know.

No need for him to be a Mason, because he holds already the most advanced views on Internationalism, and must be a source of daily delight to the Learned Elders: a Rabbi's rapture.

There was one period whilst I was at Brixton, when I thought the fiat had gone forth 'Churchill must go.' The National Press—the barometer of 'public opinion'—commenced captious criticism, but the agitation soon died down, so I can only suppose that the wrong record had been handed out, or else that the policy had been countermanded.

Churchill has told us that he did not become the King's First Minister in order to preside over the dissolution of the British Empire, but unfortunately today there are other influences, which possess greater power than the Throne, working behind the scenes.

Ever since the days of James II, the prerogative of the Crown has been whittled away, until today His Gracious Majesty has little or no control over the policy of His Ministers. This is a sad pity to those of us who believe in real Kingship, as a safeguard for national interests.

Churchill possesses many of the qualities which make a successful politician. He is a glutton for work, a fine orator, a brilliant writer, and is inspired by great courage, matchless effrontery, and an insatiable ambition and lust for power.

I read somewhere that he "wishes that life should be one great tragedy and that he himself should be in the centre of it." If that is true, he has attained his ambition in full measure.

One of my earliest recollections of Churchill is an event which must have taken place during the summer of 1912, when the Irish Home Rule trouble was seething. Winston had just been over to Ulster accompanied by his wife, and had got himself into hot water all round, for reasons which escape me.

I was attending an evening party at Sir Edgar Speyer's just after Winston's return. The huge Park Lane drawing room was filled with little groups of people standing about, engaged in conversation. Everyone of any importance in the political world was there.

I saw Winston and his wife announced, and watched them slowly progressing across the floor. He must have known nearly everybody present.

I noticed to my secret amusement that, as he approached each group, its members were so busily engaged in talking, that they had not a moment to spare for Winston. To put it plainly, he was cut all round.

He came steadily on through this barrage of snubs from an unfriendly crowd, until he reached the door where I was standing. When he saw me, his face broke into a broad grin, and he said, "I have had a pleasant evening," and out he passed with his beautiful wife on his arm, straight out of the house, after the briefest stay on record. I knew then that you could not squash that one.

I could not help admiring his *sangfroid* on a difficult occasion. He did not care twopence: he knew that this social ostracism would not last, and he had no intention of allowing it to disturb him in the least. Absolutely snub-proof. You might just as well try and stick pins into an armour plate.

I do not propose to furnish my readers with extracts from Churchillian utterances, shewing the facility and audacity with which he can box the compass of political outlook, without turning a hair, or caring a jot for the effect on his audience.

This is an accomplishment common to most of our modern politicians, who would probably call it flexibility or adaptability to changed conditions, and so on: nothing so vulgar as time-serving or sticking to office at all costs, regardless of principle. Suffice it to say, that as a political contortionist, Churchill is unequalled and unblushing.

What alarmed me far more when he became Prime Minister was the recollection of some of his strategic flights in the Great War and after, and the far greater opportunities which he now possessed.

My mind travelled back to the time when I had been an assistant Secretary at the Committee of Imperial Defence, and Churchill was at the Admiralty.

On the 3rd August, 1914, the day before war was declared, I went across to the Admiralty to collect a lighthearted plan of Winston's for landing the Expeditionary Force on the Continent: I forget where; probably in the Scheldt.

Armed with this document, I re-crossed Whitehall to the War Office, to confront Sir Henry Wilson with this effort at amateur strategy. I caught him in a bad mood, because the Government would not make up their minds how many of the six Divisions of the Expeditionary Force they could bring themselves to part with for dispatch to France.

The whole plan to the last gaiter-button had been worked out for months, and only awaited the decision of these pusillanimous old gentlemen.

When 'Ugly' Wilson saw Winston's contribution to the day's anxieties, his safety valves lifted, and he released a torrent of naughty words, which I could not have beaten myself, even when in full training in sailing-ship days. However his Irish sense of humour soon re-asserted itself, and we parted on good terms.

Winston was thwarted, but not defeated. He brought off his own plan for Antwerp with naval ratings, which some of the victims may still remember.

The Dardanelles expedition was more hopeful, but was ruined at birth by the neglect of the most golden of all the principles of war—the necessity for Surprise when landing on a defended coast.

The preliminary naval bombardment, carried out several weeks in advance, gave the enemy due notice of our intentions, from which he was not slow to profit, in making arrangements for our reception. Even with this handicap, our gallant men were within an ace of victory.

I was relieved when Winston left the Admiralty, although he managed to find plenty of outlet for his activities, especially in the various little wars going on in Russia after the 1917 Revolution.

Ever since the Great War, Mr. Churchill has been an ardent supporter of the continentalism involved in our Alliance with France, though this issue remained in the background whilst the policy of Collective Security under the League's auspices, was still supposed to retain some reality.

No statesman had appeared on the scene to guide us back to the only sound policy for a great Sea-Power—the abandonment of continental adventure: one and all were determined to stick to the blood-and-mud policy involved in European military meddling, which has sapped our great strength so grievously.

Churchill and his entourage worked hard on the flagging spirit of France, to encourage her to embark upon another struggle with Germany, instead of adopting the sensible course of trying to reach an accommodation with her powerful neighbour, the only sane long-term policy, in view of the relative rates at which their populations and national strengths were changing.

We incurred a great responsibility when we assisted to drag a reluctant Marianne to her Calvary, of which Churchill must take a big share. I do not suppose this will weigh upon him very heavily; just another milestone on the road of his boundless ambition.

Churchill is a great salesman: he has sold himself to the British Empire: that he has shaken the Empire to its foundations in the process won't lose him a moment's sleep. *Il chasse de race.* John Churchill, first Duke of Marlborough, set a very bad example in many respects.

After all, what does it matter to Winston on which side of the Atlantic the British Empire pieces are collected? This land is really too small to contain his fervent internationalism: half his heart is enshrined in that big new, Paradise across the Atlantic, whence hails the distaff side of his pedigree—or some of it.

For his energy, ruthlessness and untiring industry, in conducting modern warfare, I have nothing but admiration.

The age of chivalry is dead. Kill-as-kill-can is the order of the day: enemy, ally and neutral are equally liable to figure on the butcher's bill. Assassination is lauded, and rewarded. In these circumstances, anyone with old fashioned ideas of honour, or addicted to moral squeamishness, would be hopelessly out of place.

Churchill would brook no interference with the 'war-effort'—that magic catchword which covers every form of abomination, and which has disgraced our civilisation. To many, Churchill is enthroned as a national hero: he has certainly succeeded by his courage in extricating us from the many difficult positions in which we should never have found ourselves, but for the folly of himself and his friends.

To me, he remains what he has always been—a national calamity, as are all those who think like him.

Perhaps after the war he will pay a long trans-Atlantic visit: and take the whelp with him: and leave us to try hard to become English again.

XLIV.

Herbert Morrison, our other subject for thought, is a very different person. In many ways he is a remarkable phenomenon.

Every man is entitled to change his mind; to turn his coat; but Morrison has turned not only his coat, but his trousers and waistcoat as well—nay, his very skin itself.

In the Great War, he was one of its most vociferous opponents, discouraging his countrymen from taking part in it.

The following article from his pen appeared in the 'Labour Leader' on the 3rd September, 1914, when we were in a tight corner:—

YOUR KING AND COUNTRY NEED YOU.
(By Herbert Morrison.)
Your King and Country need you!

Ah! Men of the Country, you are remembered. Neither the King, nor the country, nor the picture papers had really forgotten you. When your master tried to cut your wages down—did you think he knew of your beautiful brave heart? When you were unemployed—did you think your country had forgotten you? When the military were used against you in the strike—did you wonder if your King was quite in love with you? Did you? . . . . Ah! Foolish one. Your King and Country need you!

Need hundreds of thousands of you to go to hell and to do the work of hell.

The Commandment says: "Thou shalt not kill." Pooh! What does it matter? Commandments, like treaties, were made to be broken. Ask your parson: he will explain.

Your King and Country need you!

Go forth, little soldier! Though you know not what you fight for—go forth! Though you have no grievance against your German brother—go forth and kill him! Though you may know he has a wife and family dependent upon him: he is only a German dog. Will he not kill you if he gets the chance? Of course he will.

He is being told the same story.

His King and Country need him."

* * * *

Well! Well! Well! And the author of this chatty little piece of sedition did not even get put in the jug for it—much less undergo more drastic treatment. No, he has lived to keep locked up for an indefinite period, men who held a somewhat more orthodox view of patriotism.

After the Great War Morrison remained consistently hostile to the provision of adequate armaments to sustain our foreign policy, and set his face firmly against any martial display that might give the youth of the country a taste for such a dreadful thing as war.

How came the fierce little warrior we know today to change his allegiance so completely from Pax to Mars? I wonder who could supply the answer—I can't. To me it remains just another riddle in the land of Topsy-Turvey.

It would have been comforting to know that one's freedom was at the nominal mercy of some more consistent individual than this political quick-change artist.

His King and Country need him—I don't think!

XLV.

Well, that is enough about the background: let us take a look at the foreground—Brixton Prison.

We left the car on its journey from Gerald Road Police Station to the haven on Brixton Hill. Alas. It was to be three long years before I could parody R. L. S. and write:—

> "Home is the sailor, home from the sea
> And the hunted home from the hill."

Jebb Avenue, the entrance to this home for hunted sailors, is a *cul-de-sac* nearly at the top of Brixton Hill. A most healthy spot. I have never been fitter than during the three years I spent there. Possibly this unsolicited testimonial may comfort those whose nearest and dearest may find themselves called upon to seek temporary seclusion in this Government non-denominational monastery.

Once safely inside the double gates of the prison, the Inspector who had brought me, led me through a door marked 'Receptions,' and handed me over to the prison authorities, receiving in exchange a Body Receipt.

Henceforth, I became a body and nothing more: presumably I parked my soul outside the gates to await the day of deliverance.

What a tale all those lost souls could tell. I only hoped that I should be handed back the right one when I left, because I had taken rather a fancy to it, and it might not suit anyone else.

During my residence I became enamoured of a Book of Forms, much used in the Prison service, labelled 'Body Receipts.'

I meant to annex one before I left, and to keep it on my hall table for the use of visitors when I got home again, but the opportunity that proverbially makes the thief, was lacking.

The door marked 'Receptions' gave me quite a nice friendly feeling: I had attended a great many receptions in my life, in various parts of the world, and although many were boring, I had some pleasant recollections. The very term implies hospitality.

Once more, alas! This was a new kind of reception altogether. I was ushered into a lobby in company with other 'Bodies,' and accommodated on a bench between two buck niggers, presumably suspected of criminal offences.

Possibly at other receptions I had been similarly situated, but at any rate it had not been quite so obvious.

Somewhat disillusioned by my reception, I sat for about an hour, before being conducted to my next port of call, designated a Reception Cell: one of the black men kindly carried my suitcase.

My new residence evokes no tender memories: it was semi-detached, a little larger than a telephone call-box, and roofed in with wire netting. It was devoid of furnishings, except for a shelf at the inner end, intended to sit upon, but barely wide enough to accommodate a well-upholstered posterior.

After being locked in, I was left to my own resources for four or five hours. I shall always remember this sojourn as the most unpleasant item in my imprisonment. The unknown future loomed darkly. There was no question of rest or meditation, as I had a very noisy neighbour who occupied his time in his interpretation of singing, and in beating upon his door.

I imagine that these retreats are intended as cooling-off places after the rush and bustle of the outer world, especially for those who have arrived with an overload of liquid fuel, whose effects would require some time to wear off.

XLVI.

I had a bottle of whisky in my bag, and I took it out and had a swig for comfort, as I was unable to Dig for Victory.

The Inspector had not discouraged the idea of the bottle accompanying me on my journey, although he must have been fully aware that spirits are forbidden in the prison world.

This particular bottle had quite a history of its own: it was the most courted bottle of whisky in the world. When the time arrived, it was duly consigned to my 'Property,' which consisted of everything I had brought with me, except the few articles permitted to accompany me on the final stages of the journey to my cell.

This property was catalogued, and then locked up in a storeroom.

On many occasions during my stay in Brixton, various Prison Officers came and reminded me about this bottle of whisky: they seemed quite anxious that I should know that it was still there, and in good health. Eventually weary of these importunities, I said that I never wanted to see it again. That was enough. I didn't. But there were many disappointed suitors; and I never discovered how its name became erased from the inventory.

Incidentally the one disability I suffered from my imprisonment was that I emerged a teetotaller.

I have always been suspicious of teetotallers, and felt no inclination to become one. In prison, however, I soon got tired of alcoholic drinks, and discontinued them, with the result that on my reappearance in the outer world, I had lost any desire to drink, and I had kept so fit, that I thought I would leave well alone.

Of course, Time, the great healer, may cure me of this disability. In any case, I want to make it quite plain, that I am not recommending prison as a cure for intemperance.

Here and now, I warn any teetotal fanatics, who may be misguided enough to invite me to appear on a platform, as a glorious example of what prison can achieve, that I shall demand a large fee for my services, in advance, and shall make a point of getting gloriously drunk on the proceeds before arriving on the platform, because I still retain a strong prejudice against any form of narrow-mindedness, in spite of setting such a bad example myself.

XLVII.

I was delighted to leave my Reception Cell, although I was only passing from Scylla to Charybdis, in the shape of yet another Cell, where I arrived as the shades of evening were drawing on.

This one was known as a Bath cell, and I was not locked up, but directed to strip, and plunge into a delousing bath, complete with carbolic soap. A notice was exhibited over the bath, stating that "Heads must be Washed."

Medical inspection, weighing, registration of valuables, and recording of 'property,' completed the preliminaries, and I was all set for the final journey, carrying the objects

I was allowed to retain in a pillow-case. I had been offered a prison-suit of clothes, but found my own more becoming, and this was permissible.

XLVIII.

I reached my home in 'F' Wing about 7:0 p.m., tired out after a glut of new experience.

These prison Blocks are gloomy affairs, consisting of a long narrow hall, with doors into the fresh air at each end, and either three or four tiers of cells on either side, extending the whole length of the building. The iron stairways to reach the upper tiers are situated half-way along the hall. A wire netting is fastened over the well of the hall, to discourage the inmates from dropping bricks from the upper regions upon any heads they may not fancy.

Abreast the stairways on every floor is a recess bisecting the long rows of cells. This recess contains one water-closet with a half-door denying privacy, a sink for discharging slops, and a cold water tap. My cell was on the Ground Floor, adjoining the recess.

'F' Wing was an old building, long disused for prisoners, and condemned as unfit for service: it had been re-opened for our benefit. Here were housed those individuals who had not yet visited the Advisory Committee: they were kept carefully segregated from those who had already had their interviews, presumably in order to prevent them gaining any slight experience which might benefit them in their one-sided contest with the Tribunal, of which more anon.

The cells are mainly distinguished by their architectural simplicity, and omission of any protuberance which might assist a world-weary occupant to try and end his mental suspense by an act of physical suspension, leading to a better world.

The cell doors were ancient contraptions, with a very noisy and clumsy locking apparatus. In each door was the customary Judas-hole, the flap being operated from the outside. A dim electric light was attached to the roof, barely sufficient to read by, and also operated from outside the cell. The lighting is on a low voltage system, to avoid any temptation to electrocution.

The barred windows consisted of tiny panes, only one of which could be opened to admit air through an aperture about seven inches by five.

A hot air system for heating the cells in cold weather was fitted.

The cell furniture comprised a plank bed about two inches from the ground, stowed on edge by day against the wall; a small wooden table and chair, a triangular wooden wash-hand-stand, with enamelled iron basin, jug, soap-dish and mug, all in varying stages of battered antiquity; an enamelled iron chamber-pot, complete (or not) with lid, a thick porcelain plate and mug, and a knife which was not a knife, but a paper-cutter of antique design.

A couple of small shelves were fixed in one corner: a row of diminutive knobs for the suspension of towel and plate-cloth completed a drab ensemble.

XLIX.

By the time I arrived, my companions in misfortune were safely locked up for the night, but a Debtor prisoner, of whom a few were attached to each Wing for cleaning purposes, helped me make my unaccustomed bed.

I stowed my few effects on the two small shelves, and was only too glad to be locked up, and to try and sleep after an unusually hectic twenty-four hours. I was not very successful in wooing slumber, and I disliked being so close to the concrete floor.

When I became more knowing, I supported my plank-bed at its two ends on the chair and table lying on their sides.

This gave a certain amount of spring to an uncomfortable platform, besides raising me from the dingy floor.

The chair lying on its side had another useful function to perform, when its rungs gripped the rim of my chamber-pot, forming a dainty little cabin *lieu d'aisance*.

One glance at the water-closet in the Recess had convinced me that for the duration of my captivity, I must return to my nursery habits in this respect: it was a choice of evils.

However, as Burke tells us, custom reconciles us to everything, and I was soon qualified to be hereditary pot-bearer to the Governor of Brixton Prison.

No trim parlourmaid in a print dress called me on my first morning at Brixton, with a nice cup of tea.

At 6:45 a.m. the cell door clanged open, and a warder —I beg his pardon, prison officer—bawled out "Slop out: hurry up there." Thus was I introduced to one of the Cries of London, not well known to the general public, but very familiar to the habitués of its gaols.

One of my guardians during my early days at Brixton had served under me as a petty officer when I was afloat. He had been lent temporarily from Chelmsford Prison, owing to the press of 18B business. When he opened a cell door one fine morning, and saw his recent and highly esteemed admiral berthed inside, he thought for a moment that he was seeing things. I quickly disillusioned him, and assured him that his eyesight was all right: it was only one of his naval deities that was lying shattered at his feet.

Poor chap, he never quite recovered from this shock, and was glad to return to Chelmsford shortly for a rest-cure, and a glimpse of a few honest-to-God convicts.

At first we were not supposed to emerge for the morning slop-out unless fully dressed: no dressing gowns or other fripperies were allowed. Gradually we broke down a lot of adhesions in the prison routine, but it was a long and weary process.

The trouble was that an 18B was a new type of animal, hitherto unknown to the Prison Zoo, and, failing instructions to the contrary, we were treated in the same manner as the more common species—the Remand Biped, or Brixtonia Ordinaris.

This was not the fault of the Prison authorities who were quite ready to oblige, but, unfortunately, they were under the thumb of a Special Division of clerks, collected together at the Home Office to administer 18B.

I presume that these clerks carried out their duties in accordance with their instructions, but the results, as far as the victims were concerned, were most unpleasant.

They made life as uncomfortable for us as possible; any indignities and inconveniences that could be devised, were supplied. Presumably they acquired good marks from higher authority, who did not attempt to tamper with the prison staff direct, as far as I could discover, but I cannot be sure.

Speaking for myself only, I never had anything but the most pleasant relations with the Prison Officers.

Many of them had been in the fighting Services, which helped.

They carried out a difficult and uncongenial job, to the best of their ability. Naturally some were a bit rougher than others; the prison service hardly lends itself to gentle ways, but, taken by and large, they were a very good lot of fellows, and some of them I liked immensely.

It was to be expected that their treatment of us when we first arrived was very different to what it was later on, when they realised a little better what was in the wind, and that we were not the bold, bad men that they had been led to expect, but only the victims of a political persecution very alien to this country.

L.

Our day's routine in " F " Wing was as follows: after being let out at 6:45 a.m. for the morning slop-out, we were locked up until breakfast was brought round at 7:15, when we were locked up again to enjoy it. At 9:00 o'clock we were enlarged for another slop-out, and then locked up until 9:30, when we went into the fresh air for exercise.

This consisted in marching round a grass plot on a narrow stone pavement for an hour, after which 'association' was allowed—nothing to do with football, but merely another term peculiar to prison life, or rather with a particular interpretation.

In practice, it meant sitting about on our wooden chairs, reading or playing cards, or doing anything else in reason that one liked in the playground.

Indoors again at 11:30 and locked up: dinner at 11:40, after which we remained locked up until just before 2 p.m.

then we went outside again until 3:30. The final meal arrived about 4:00, when we were locked up for the night, except for an uncertain 'slop-out' about 6:30 p.m.

Lights went out at 9 p.m., or earlier, if there was an air-raid on.

During these raids, of which there were many during the early months, we were always locked up, being brought indoors if necessary, so that we often spent as much as 23 hours out of 24 in solitary confinement, with a minimum of 19 1/2 hours, if there were no raid, and things were going well.

LI.

A tedious life for those unable to support their own company, but I soon got acclimatized to the strange conditions, as I was quite determined that nothing should upset me. I always felt extremely sorry for those who suffered from claustrophobia, especially during air raids, which must have been an agony to them. These were occasions when deafness was an advantage, as I slept peacefully through all the turmoil, only being awakened in a few instances when my bed was badly shaken by a bomb falling rather unpleasantly close to the prison.

Anyone taken ill at night was also much to be pitied. The only way of attracting attention was to press a knob in the wall near the door, which sprang a rattler and pushed out an iron indicator to shew the nightwatchman, an aged man with muffled feet, who was disturbing the peace. He had no cell-keys, but could only telephone across to the Centre after ascertaining by shouting through the door, what was the trouble.

Not a very satisfactory arrangement for a nervous invalid, and it was not surprising that one or two poor fellows lost all control of themselves.

I only had one nocturnal alarm myself, when one of the prison cats elected to spend the remainder of the night with me, after his evening rounds. He crawled through the tiny window space, and took a flying leap on to my bed in the dark. That did make me jump. He settled down comfortably at my feet, and evidently found my bed so much to his liking, that he returned on several occasions. I was glad to have his company, once I had ascertained the nature of my visitor. A large rat would not have been so welcome, as you knew only too well that there was no means of getting rid of him again.

Many of the cells were infested with bugs, which made their homes in the bed-boards and chairs. Some of my comrades were badly bitten in this way, and I considered myself fortunate to be lacking in bug-appeal.

My only affliction was caused by the unyielding nature of the pillow, which made my ears sore. Later on, I put this right with a pillow from home. I forgot rheumatism, a very common prison malady, but this vanished when I used—well, a much advertised remedy. (N.B. No manufacturers need apply).

The linen was coarse, but good: clean sheets once a month. The blankets varied in warmth and cleanliness, but a little importunity put this right. The coloured prison rugs made a cheerful addition, and gave one a pardonable glow of pride, as they were made by fellow-sufferers in some of the prisons.

LII.

As regards food, we were allowed to order our meals from an outside caterer. The longer I stayed in Prison, the more I adopted the prison menu, which was good in many respects, especially after one of our Governors had devised a more appetising way of serving dinners than out of the ordinary metal containers, which are unpleasant looking things.

I do not pretend that I should like to have been confined to the monotony of the prison diet, but supplemented by odds and ends from home, things were not too bad. Don't imagine that we were living at a Mayfair, or even a Soho, standard, but merely that food was far from being the worst feature of prison life.

I was glad of our forethought in starting a poultry-yard at our little home in Roehampton. The pullets started to lay shortly after my wife and I commenced our rest-cures, as if in sympathy with our affliction, and right well did they accomplish their war-work. The eggs arrived at the prison hard-boiled, but so was I, so that was all right.

The national egg policy had developed in the meantime on the lines of the jam policy at the Mad Hatter's teaparty, where you will recollect that the rule was "Jam tomorrow and Jam yesterday, but never Jam today."

Food from outside sources was subject at first to some tiresome regulations. We were not allowed to have anything in tin or glass containers, presumably to remove aids to escape or suicide, the two prison bugbears: I never discovered which was regarded as the more serious offence. We had attempts at both.

Potted meat was not nearly so appetising after being removed from its jar, and screwed up in a bit of paper by a prison officer; nor was port wine, matured in a prison billy can.

Milk and Jam appeared in cartons. Later on all these restrictions were removed. Perhaps they had assisted in turning me into a disciple, I hope temporary, of Lady Astor.

I always hoped that the following story anent this good lady was true, although I am sure it isn't: it is too good to be true.

She is reputed to have got so warmed up to her work on a temperance platform as to say, "Do you know, I really believe that sooner than drink a glass of beer, I would rather commit adultery." A voice from the audience spoilt the effect of this dubious thesis, by remarking audibly "Who wouldn't?"

LIII.

Two of the restrictions to which I never paid any attention were those in connection with watches and razor blades.

To be deprived of one's watch is a great bore to anyone as deaf as I am, when locked up all round the clock.

Just at first, I had no means whatever of knowing what hour of the day or night we had reached, except the rough indications given by those crude time-pieces, the stomach and the sun.

I couldn't hear any of the chiming clocks, which were within listening range of those not suffering from my disability.

I imported my wrist watch at a very early date, and later on a cheap Swiss watch, as my own chronometer was in my 'property,' and therefore out of reach.

My daughter Miranda, who came to visit me, was a most accomplished smuggler, and I was none too bad myself. In spite of the strict surveillance of our visits, we managed to do quite a lot of sleight-of-hand, and were proud of our achievements.

How appropriately Shakespeare's Miranda says:—

"It would become me as well as it does you
And I should do it with much more ease."

Had we been caught *in flagrante delicto* I do not believe we should have been severely treated, as my daughter was very popular with the prison officers, who were always asking me when 'Miranda' was coming.

I caused some amusement at a much later date when the Governor fell us all in to tell us of the gracious concession made by the Home Secretary in allowing us to have our watches; I produced mine out of my pocket forthwith, so pleased was I at having no further need of snatching furtive glances at this forbidden luxury.

Needless to say, I would never have allowed any of the prison officers to get into trouble over my misdemeanours, if I could possibly have avoided it. Fortunately this difficulty did not arise.

Razor blades were kept in a box in the hall, under the Desk Officer's eye, and only allowed to be removed for immediate use, and then returned. I never took any notice of this order, and made certain that I could shave when I wanted to, by keeping my own supply.

Of course there were numerous cell-searchings, but one developed the old lag's cunning very quickly.

LIV.

We were a very mixed bag in 'F' Wing; about two hundred of us, as far as I can remember: nominally all British subjects, but many of foreign origin on one or both sides, especially Italian or German as was only to be expected.

You could take your choice from prince to pimp, brothel-keepers, con-men, members of race-course gangs, bookies, professional boxers, naval, military and air force officers and men, bankers and other representatives of commerce and business, professional men and all kinds of manual workers.

No matter what their job, men were ruthlessly immured in these days of panic. Ministers of religion were reft from their flocks; schoolmasters gave their pupils an unexpected holiday; doctors and dentists left their patients to their aches and pains. Many men saw their life's work swept away, and their families forced to accept poor relief. Had they only had the good fortune to be enemy aliens, their affairs would have been looked after for them by the Government: being British subjects, their interests were allowed to go to rack and ruin.

National Security was pleaded for these activities, but there is something strangely reminiscent of them in the Protocols.

I derived much amusement from one elderly gentleman of Italian origin, who was frankly terrified of Air Raids, and invented his own Air Raid Precautions.

By day, he sat at the table in his cell under an inverted 'V,' formed by his bed-boards and mattress: by night, he lay on his mattress underneath his bed-boards, with his chamber-pot reversed slung over his head as armour protection. He was proud of his ingenuity, and invited his neighbours to inspect the results.

LV.

Our numbers were largely reduced when the various prison camps were opened; in addition, to relieve the pressure, many 18B prisoners had the misfortune to be sent to other prisons.

Liverpool enjoyed a particularly evil reputation for ill-treatment. Some of the stories I was told made my blood boil, and those individuals who had had the good fortune to be sent back to Brixton, bore on their faces the unmistakable traces of the hardships they had undergone.

Bear in mind all the time that none of these men had been accused of anything, or were going to be accused of anything: no charges were ever preferred against them: in the eyes of the law they were innocent men.

One common link bound the majority together: they had incurred the enmity of the Jews.

For some time the prisoners were made to wear handcuffs during the General Post from prison to camp, and back again. In this way father was secured to son, officer to private. One clergyman was paraded round Euston Station handcuffed to a companion, and quite a crowd collected to see this unusual sight. Somebody must have given the orders for this treatment; however, a question in the House put an end to this particular indignity.

Eventually the camps at Ascot, York and Heyton were all closed, and the inmates sent to Peel in the Isle of Man. Brixton remained the Mecca of 18B's, and a few of us stayed there the whole time. I never discovered whether this was because we were regarded as really dangerous men, or whether some other motive lay behind the arrangement. I should strongly have resented being deported to the Isle of Man, and was quite content to be considered anything my captors fancied, provided they left me in peace.

LVI.

I have already referred to the third degree examination station maintained at Latchmere House, Ham Common, where selected unfortunates spent a month or more. It appears to have been a very amateur affair, which never got beyond solitary confinement, and other of the less violent forms of unpleasantness.

It was a pity Judmas did not consult some of its Ogpu friends, as it might have greatly improved its technique in attempting to extract information. I fear it must have discovered a large quantity of mare's nests, and little else.

LVII.

And so the lovely summer of 1940 slipped away, whilst we lived our unpleasant life amidst the bed-boards and the bugs.

Our one chance of escape lay through the Advisory Committee, appointed by the Home Secretary, concerning whose functions we knew little; later on, we were both sadder and wiser.

However at that time, we had great hopes of its assistance, and nearly all applied for interviews.

After a while I got tired of waiting, and was granted a writ of Habeas Corpus, with a view to hastening matters.

As a result, I was bidden to appear before the Committee at the Berystede Hotel, Ascot, where the Committee had taken refuge, when the bombing got unpleasant in London.

The High Court Judge gave permission for the hearing of my Writ to be postponed: at a much later date, he allowed me to withdraw it. I did this as soon as judgment had been given in the House of Lords in another 18B case, to the effect that the Home Secretary's affidavit that he had 'Reasonable Causes' for interning people for an indefinite period, was sufficient in law to make the detention legal. I was not going into Court for the pleasure of hearing that Mr. Morrison's word was accepted, whilst my own affidavit was ignored. I felt that that would have been more than I was called upon to bear.

LVIII.

On the 22nd October, a lovely autumn day, I drove down to Ascot.

I had been three and a half months in prison, but that was a short time to wait compared to some of my less fortunate comrades.

The last time I had taken the same road I had been accompanied by my daughter. We were arrayed in all our finery as guests of His Majesty in the Royal Enclosure for the annual meeting.

Well, I was still a guest of His Majesty, although in a less attractive capacity, and I could not help being struck by the curious turn in the Wheel of Fortune between 1939 and 1940.

On arrival at the hotel premises, I was parked in the stables to await my call to the Committee, which held its sittings in the hotel proper.

The proceedings of this Committee are one of the most unsavoury episodes in the history of England: they were apparently instituted to give the public the impression that we were getting a square deal: a great waste of effort, as the public were far too apathetic to worry about the matter.

They are always ready to trust the Government, if they think about such things at all.

I shall always regret that I appeared before the Committee. The knowing ones stood aloof, but the majority, hoping in vain for the best, made their bow to this unorthodox tribunal.

Nobody would have believed that individuals would be confined *sine die,* to gratify the vindictiveness of other individuals or parties, on the plea of national security. A lot of the pretence might have been omitted. Few would have attempted to discover what was behind this dirty business; the majority would have accepted the Home Secretary's word that he had 'reasonable causes,' without all the chicanery involved in pretending that the prisoners were getting a fair hearing.

All this circumlocution entailed the secrecy in which the proceedings of the Committee were wrapped. The prisoner was allowed no legal assistance: no companion of any sort, to bear witness to this odd justice.

The whole system was strongly reminiscent of that adopted for the Bastille prisoners in the French Revolution, where Judmas was behind the scenes.

LIX.

For the information of the many who are unacquainted with Defence Regulation 18B, it may be as well to mention that the Home Secretary was thereby enabled under a *lettre de cachet* to imprison indefinitely any persons suspected of hostile association, of acts prejudicial to national security, or of being members of Sir Oswald Mosley's political Party, British Union.

A blank cheque of unlimited scope. The prisoners were allowed to appeal against their arbitrary arrest, by stating their case before an Advisory Committee appointed by their gaoler.

The proceedings of the Committee were wrapped in the most profound secrecy.

The victims were supposed to be supplied in advance of their hearing, with particulars of the allegations made against them, so as to enable them to prepare their defence.

In practice, the 'particulars' contained innocuous material, whose disclosure could do no harm, nor give the show away; in some cases hair-raising suspicions were included, which the prisoner would be reluctant to shew to his acquaintances.

The details upon which he was actually questioned, covered a much wider field, of which the Least Common Denominator in the majority of cases was the Jewish questtion: often carefully wrapped up, but there nevertheless.

The Chairmen of the various Committees were lawyers of repute, skilled in the forensic art.

The victim was asked a string of questions, at the end of which, he was invited to make a statement. No evidence was either produced or given: no witness called. The prisoner was not allowed to know who had testified against him, although in some cases he was enabled to guess, especially when the informant was after his job or his best girl.

Having been deprived on arrest of the property relating to his case, he was unable to support his own statement by documents or other aids: the Crown, on the other hand, could make a selection of the exhibits most suitable for their case, whilst withholding those that might help the prisoner.

A shocking breach of legal decency occurred when Captain Ramsay brought a libel action against a New York newspaper, claiming heavy damages. The Defence was given access to all Captain Ramsay's effects, which had been impounded on his arrest by the Government authorities. Presumably the freemasonry of the Law allowed this scandalous procedure.

It was a grand opportunity for that despicable creature, the anonymous letter-writer, as well as for the army of secret informants and agents-provocateurs employed by the Secret Service.

These were drawn from all ranks of society, including some of the hostesses during the London season, who repeated the remarks made by their juvenile guests under the stimulus of champagne, possibly contributed by the Secret Service.

To such depths had we fallen: a queer business altogether, which can be summed up in one word—un-English, at any rate in modern times.

In our past history we had had recourse to these questionable methods, in times of unrest; they are quite unreliable, since there are no limits to the imagination of the enthusiastic agent-provocateur.

The wretched prisoner debilitated by months of imprisonment, was confronted with this odd array of 'evidence,' with no one to hold his hand or give him advice; just sitting birds to Learned Counsel. The prisoner was allowed no copy of the alleged proceedings of this precious Committee, as this would obviously have blown the whole gaff.

Two examples in my own case will suffice to illustrate the type of evidence with which we had to contend: I only heard of them after my release.

(1) A servant whom we had had to dismiss for partaking too freely of the liquid contents of the sideboard, organised a local petition, demanding that my wife and I should be removed too—to prison. Presumably she felt that the cellaret would be happier still under complete

prohibition, rather than under the partial and one-sided restrictions from which she had suffered.

(2) A brother officer, whom I barely knew, and whom I had always avoided, as I did not like the cut of his jib, as we say in the navy, asked Morrison to shut me up tighter and longer, as his wife triumphantly informed a friend of mine.

My only communication with him in post-naval years was on an occasion when I had to remonstrate strongly with him for applying the proxy votes of a certain Association of which, at the time, he was Chairman, to purposes for which they had never been intended.

I know nothing of business standards or methods, but I was quite sure that the only business in which we had been jointly connected—the Royal Navy—would not have approved of this manipulation.

Probably my views, which he himself had invited, rankled.

What a chance 18B gave to a man like this; a thoroughly patriotic proxy.

I bear no malice to this precious and imaginative couple: I feel only a vast contempt for them. I prefer the servant.

LX.

My Committee consisted of Mr. Norman Birkett (later Sir Norman Birkett, a High Court Judge), Sir George Clerk, and Sir Arthur Hazlerigg.* Mr. Birkett had been my Counsel on one occasion in a lawsuit, in which I was reluctantly involved as Executor of a Will: Sir George Clerk was a distinguished diplomat, whom I had known in the past, and Sir Arthur Hazlerigg bore a name famous in English history, in Commonwealth days.

I faced this trio across the table; my equerry from the prison sat just behind me.

The only 'offence' which could be justly laid at my door was that I was strongly opposed to the war, which I considered then, and consider still, was in the worst possible interests of the Empire, for the reasons already recorded.

---

* Now Lord Hazlerigg.

Holding these views, I founded the 'Link,' and worked hard and successfully at its non-political activities.

If this was a crime, then I am guilty; and proud of it.

Incidentally friendship with Germany was also the ostensible policy of the Government, when I founded the 'Link,' although I admit that does not afford much guarantee of continuity, when Judmas is behind the scenes.

My examination only lasted just over an hour, and passed off very pleasantly. I told the Committee that I felt like a man arrested for murder, and charged nearly four months later with petty larceny. I am afraid I must have been a bitter disappointment to Judmas, who had hoped for something much more sensational, having judged me by its own standards of morality.

When I left the Committee, to my great surprise and joy, I met my wife for luncheon, as Mr. Birkett had thoughtfully arranged to see us both on the same day.

It was the first time I had set eyes upon her since we had parted in Gerald Road Police Station, and she looked as if she had weathered the storm as well as I had.

We compared notes over our meal, and agreed that we had both had a good run for our money before the Committee, although three and a half months had been a long time to wait for the pleasure of an interview.

Our boy came over from the camp at Ascot to see us, so we had a real red letter day in the life of 18B's.

LXI.

On my return to Brixton, I went into 'C' Wing to join the other post-graduates of English Justice in the twentieth century.

This was a much more comfortable proposition than 'F' Wing; I had a bed complete with springs, and quite a large portion of the window opened to admit fresh air. The floor was tiled. Altogether a very Ritzy affair.

I found myself next door to Sir Oswald Mosley on the first floor, or C2 landing in prison reckoning. Our windows overlooked the exercise yard for Remand prisoners; we could thus inspect the daily bag, having their morning constitutional before setting out for the various courts and assizes.

This was my home for nearly three years.

LXII.

On 5th November—a very suitable day—my wife and I were unexpectedly recalled before the Committee.

The atmosphere had deteriorated since our last visit. The barometer was no longer 'Set Fair' but 'Stormy.'

I had the feeling that I was no longer being treated as a timid witness being conducted through his examination-in-chief, but rather as a stubborn, hostile witness.

Something must have gone wrong in the interval; perhaps they had been given the wrong riding instructions in the first instance: now they had to pull a winning horse. ("Will the horse win," said the anxious backer. "Yes, if the reins break," replied the candid jockey). On comparing notes again, my wife and I agreed that we had backed a loser, and we boded no good from this second visit. Our instinct was correct; early in December we were told that we should be 'further detained.'

It is very unsatisfactory not to be told the verdict of the Committee, nor the grounds upon which further detention is ordered. The Home Secretary is not bound by the finding of the Committee, and admits to consulting all sorts of outside authorities, with a finger in the pie; this is all part of the general hocus-pocus, but I have little doubt that Judmas was the real arbiter of one's fate as an 18B.

It would be nice to know definitely who to thank for this prolonged extension of Government hospitality. I was well brought up, and like to be able to send a 'bread-and-butter' letter at the end of my visit.

LXIII.

I decided to make myself as comfortable as possible for a voyage of such uncertain length. A few cushion covers turned my bed into quite a presentable sofa in the daytime, helped out with a rug and so on. Various other knick-knacks made the place more homely. In fact my cell became quite a cabin, and was much admired by various visitors, invited and otherwise.

We began to break down a lot of the restrictions, which had never been meant to apply to us.

It was weary uphill work; sometimes it was within the Governor's jurisdiction; sometimes the matter had to go to the Home Office, or to the Prison Commissioners. By degrees, we were left unlocked for longer and longer periods, and after a prolonged fight, we got permission to have our lights on until 10 p.m., a welcome concession from our little Hitlers.

The only channel of communication which the Home Office had forgotten to block, or had not ventured to do so, was the one leading to members of Parliament.

A few of the latter interested themselves in our plight, and were helpful in getting our restrictions removed. I am sure all the members of the 18B Club will remember the work of Sir Irving Albery and his colleagues with gratitude.

They found it a thankless task, as Morrison resented interference. I presume his masters took him to task if he eased things up too much.

Some of us were actually allowed to dine together on Christmas night, in a double cell adjacent to mine, a great dissipation.

LXIV.

The first winter was very cold. We had no hot water in ' C ' Wing, as the Office of Works reported that the small boiler supplied for the purpose, was cracked and unsafe for use.

We had to do all our washing, shaving and washing-up of dirty cups and plates in cold water.

It struck me as a curious feature of prison life, that the Governor of the establishment appeared to have no jurisdiction over some parts of the ship's company; both the doctors and the staff from the Office of Works ploughed lonely, and sometimes very crooked, furrows.

It would be impossible to run a ship, if the Captain had not got the 'Assassins' and the plumbers under his thumb.

Cases of dispute have been known on board ship, where it became a contest between the principal medical officer and the captain, as to which could put the other *hors-de-combat* first, the former by placing the latter on the sick list, before the latter could put the former under arrest.

However, that is by the way. One young 18B of an inventive turn of mind, devised a simple stove out of an old tobacco tin, a lump of margarine for fuel, and a piece of string for wick: crude but moderately efficient, and he presented me with an early model, from which I produced a strong smell and a little heat.

I was not surprised when the news leaked out, and one of the prison officers came and told me that there was going to be a stove raid, and advised me to get rid of mine.

I ignored this well-meant warning, saying that I intended to take my share of the blame.

The raid duly took place, and I was ordered to appear before the Governor. This entailed being locked into my cell, and visited by the doctor, to see that I was physically fit for any punishment the Governor might see fit to inflict.

Later on I was unlocked and escorted into the Presence. By this time I was feeling fairly explosive.

I told the poor man that he knew full well that I had made a point of never complaining about his beastly prison, but I did not wish him to gather from that, that I had no grounds for complaint. I gave him a few examples, including the lack of hot water, and told him that I preferred to use my lump of margarine for warming water, rather than for poisoning my inside. Altogether I quite enjoyed this opportunity of blowing off steam.

I was followed by Captain Ramsay, another offender on the same charge, and I have no doubt that he gave the

Governor some of the eloquence he was unable to expend on the House of Commons.

As a result, we had hot water from a miraculously recovered boiler the next morning.

Thus ended what came to be known as the battle of the Grease Lamps: it was fought in January, 1941.

LXV.

For some time Sir Oswald Mosley and I had been seeking permission to visit our wives in Holloway prison.

The negotiations with the Home Office dragged on in the usual way; they could not make up their minds whether to let us go at all, and, in the event of approval, how often, and for what length of time.

Sad experience of Government Offices made me realise that something drastic was needed to force a decision, the one thing Authority seeks to avoid, in the pleasant paper game played in Whitehall, where passing the buck is the orthodox move.

The 9th of February, 1941 was my Silver Wedding day, and I suggested that this would be a suitable day for such a startling innovation.

This gave much anxious thought to the little Masons at the Home Office. However it was effective, and on the appointed day, Sir Oswald and I drove across London, heavily escorted, to see our respective spouses in Holloway gaol. A great event. I cannot help thinking that a Silver Wedding celebration in prison must be a world's record, if not a very enviable one.

We were allowed half an hour on this occasion, later extended to one hour, on our fortnightly visits: not a long time to justify such elaborate route arrangements.

It is no fun being a dangerous man: I suppose it was necessary to keep up all this pretence; the clerks probably enjoyed it, and thereby justified their existence.

I was relieved to find that the conditions for all the poor women shut up by these political sadists were much less onerous than ours, but the whole thing was a very

FROM ADMIRAL TO CABIN BOY

black blot on the escutcheon of the once chivalrous English. If insistence on the vote brought the poor creatures to this, I expect many would have willingly foregone it.

There were women in Holloway, who had been forcibly fed before the last war, for their political agitation: they must feel today like real war veterans. Shame on British Manhood!

These fortnightly visits made a very pleasant break in prison monotony; some 18B prisoners returned from the Isle of Man, so that they could avail themselves of this privilege: perhaps privilege is hardly the word to use, when the whole business was such a crying scandal.

LXVI.

If anyone wants to know what it is like being in prison, I can only reply that everyone makes what he likes of it, and that my experiences and reactions are of little value to anyone else, who must buy his experience, not on the bookstall, but in the hard school of trial and effect.

Personally I found prison life far from irksome. I have always been a great reader which helps a lot. There is plenty of interest in life, however it is spent, if you know where to find it.

Nothing I say here is meant to condone the action of the politicians who sent us to prison: I hope to see them brought to book some day: what a Rogues' Gallery we shall have.

Evelyn Waugh wrote an amusing satire called 'A Decline and Fall," in which the hero goes to gaol, and records his experiences.

Many a true word is spoken in jest, and I hope the gifted author will pardon me for giving extracts from his work, which is not founded on his personal experience.

Part III, Chapter 1:—"The next four weeks of solitary confinement were amongst the happiest of Paul's life. The physical comforts were certainly meagre, but at the Ritz Paul had learned to appreciate the inadequacy of purely physical comfort.

"It was so exhilarating he found, never to have to make any decision on any subject, to be wholly relieved from the smallest consideration of time, meals or clothes, to have no anxiety even about what kind of impression he was making: in fact, to be free.

"A t some rather chilly time in the early morning a bell would ring, and the warder would say "Slops outside:" he would rise, roll up his bedding and dress; there was no need to shave, no hesitation about what tie he should wear, none of the fidgeting with studs and collars and links that so distracts the waking moments of civilised man. He felt like the happy people in the advertisements for shaving soap who seem to have achieved very simply that peace of mind so distant and so desirable in the early morning."

Part III, Chapter IV:—. . . . . "for anyone who has been to an English public school will always feel comparatively at home in prison. It is the people brought up in the gay intimacy of the slums, Paul learned, who find prison so soul destroying."

There is a great deal of truth in the foregoing extracts written in a jesting vein, except that I do not believe that anyone would like *real* solitary confinement; but I doubt if the author means that ordeal, judging by the context.

If you do not get bored by your own company, you are afforded ample quiet opportunities for developing your mind which are unobtainable to the majority in the bustle of every day life in the modern world.

Whilst unlikely to suffer from prison nostalgia like the Dartmoor shepherd of Churchill fame, I have been in many worse spots than Brixton gaol, and that is a lot for a man who loves his own home to say.

I should like to add to Evelyn Waugh's list of worries mercifully denied to a prisoner, Fleet Street at the front door and Fleet Street on the telephone, two of the greatest trials in modern life for a man who willy-nilly has become 'news.' It really was a joy to be quit of these twin pests for a while.

LXVII.

Our exercise ground in 'C' Wing was roomy and pleasant, judged by prison standards. In the fine, warm weather, we could sit about and read, and we even arranged an outdoor 'silent room,' so dear to the club habitué.

We had many a jolly game of cricket and rounders. Although I had never risen much above the standard of village cricket in the outer world, I found that my prison status with a tennis ball was considerably higher: with all due modesty I claim to have attained county form in prison cricket. I developed a late cut which placed the ball down the coal-basement, which I heard compared favourably with Ranji and Bobby Abel at their best, although jealous Etonians of whom we boasted several, described it as a 'Harrow drive.'

Captain Ramsay, one of these Etonians, temporarily absolved from attendance at Westminster, coached eager disciples from Soho and Shepherd's Market, and greatly raised the Brixton standard of cricket.

It was a treat to see Captain Gordon Canning, another Etonian, lift a half-volley over Lenin's tomb (the Recreation ground lavatories) into the Fire tank—quite as good as one over the Pavilion at Lord's.

The ball often sailed over the prison wall, and I should like to pay a tribute to the decency of the people who returned it, in these days of shortage.

LXVIII.

Many people found the life unbearable; one long torture. It is mainly a question of temperament and health, and I can never be thankful enough for being granted such good health.

There was certainly no temptation to fall ill and pay a visit to the prison hospital.

I have no pleasant recollection of the prison doctors, and although I did not fall into their clutches, I saw enough of their system to make me thankful that I had avoided it. It was intolerably burdensome, even in small matters.

On one occasion I wanted an aperient. The humble Cascara reposed in my 'Property' and was 'verboten.'

To obtain this simple nostrum, I was locked into my cell—the invariable preliminary to any incident in prison —when I might have been out in the fresh air at exercise, to await the arrival of the doctor, whose times of call were beautifully uncertain.

One had many opportunities of studying patience in prison.

The doctor prescribed a noxious-looking potion, which arrived later in a cracked and chipped porcelain container.

After this early experience, I arranged for the supply of elementary medical comforts through my invaluable contraband service. These were much in demand; I became a dispenser in a small way myself.

My thoughts went back to the old days in torpedo-boat destroyers, where every captain was his own medico, and was assisted by a medicine chest and an omniscient coxswain.

On joining the flotilla, I asked a brother officer of greater experience, how he made his diagnosis. "Quite simple," he replied; "I draw a line across the patient's middle with my finger, and ask him if the pain is above or below that line. If above, I give him a vomito; if below, a purgito." A great contrast to the prison ways, though possibly only suited to those with the constitutions of the old seamen.

I spent a day or two in bed with the common or garden cold, but managed to stay in my cell.

I suppose the prison doctor has always to be on his guard against malingering and other dodges, which assist to make him hard-hearted and unsympathetic, and lacking in a pretty bedside manner.

LXIX.

We had a weekly bath in the prison bath-house, which held a dozen at a time. Not too bad: one of the debtors was responsible for its cleanliness.

On one occasion, the temporary guardian asked me sympathetically in a stage whisper, when I was going up for trial: he had mistaken me for an elderly member of the National Fire Service, some of whom had found their way to Brixton, on a charge of stripping the lead off the roof of London Bridge station, and other speculations, after an Air Raid. I was sorry to disappoint him; news is treasured in prison.

LXX.

The debtor system is a curious anomaly of our legal code, and a disgrace to our civilisation: but for my visit to Brixton, I should never have known it existed.

Most people are under the delusion that imprisonment for debt is obsolete: but there is a catch in this.

These poor chaps are sent to prison for contempt of Court, in refusing to comply with a Court order to pay certain sums.

The maximum sentence at one time is three months.

Many of these debtors are highly respectable men: I had a very nice London bus-driver in the cell next to mine on one occasion.

The majority of cases are those of men who, for some reason or another, refuse to support their wives: in most cases of this nature, the unfortunate man has the misfortune to be allied to a lady aptly referred to by Shakespeare, as a bed-swerver.

A little jeweller told me of his troubles, which are typical of many others. He had caught his wife *in flagrante delicto* with his own nephew, and had rather naturally booted her out. He had spent a considerable portion of his savings in trying to get a divorce, but had failed for lack of corroborative evidence. As he was legally responsible for this woman's maintenance, when she sued him, he was ordered to pay, and refused. Result; closure of the jeweller's shop, and a trip to Brixton, recurring at regular intervals.

What puzzled me was, who gained by this iniquitous system?

Certainly not the Government, who had to keep him, the debtor who had to close his shop, or the erring wife, except so far as she had satisfied her vindictiveness.

A debtor could always get out of prison by payment of the balance of his debt, which he was working off at the rate of so much a day. One man I knew always paid for a twenty-four hours rebate of sentence, so as to avoid a meeting with his wife, who had a nasty habit of coming to the prison gates to jeer at him, on the day upon which his release was due, in normal circumstances.

Another man, who was a great character, came to me in a rage one day, to announce his immediate departure. He had told me previously that he was not due for release until five days later, so I asked him what had happened to make him change his mind so suddenly. It turned out that a well-meaning 18B had told him that if he was short of a job when he got out, his wife would find him a day's work, and give him his dinner and five shillings.

The insult lay in the paltry five bob, so, in order to shew that he was a man of means above such petty considerations, he paid twenty-six bob for the early door.

He never returned to us, so I hope he took my advice about his wife, who appeared to be a tiresome lady.

These debtors wear a brown suit, instead of the convicted man's grey, two-piece costume. They are employed on odd jobs, such as cleaning the Wings, and tidying-up the grounds.

The whole business is stupid and irrational, and needs a thorough investigation, to see if some more sensible method cannot be found, for dealing with these men.

Perhaps Israel and Rebecca will find a way out, in the New Jerusalem they are planning for us. When Rebecca has obtained equal rights for both sexes by means of her Blanket Bill, these little troubles may disappear, and both husband and wife will equally incur liabilities or disabilities by neglect of the marriage bed.

I shall regret my sojourn in Brixton prison still less, if it serves to call attention to this odd method of dealing with unhappy marriages, which brings prison as a reward to the innocent partner of an adulterous wife.

Incidentally the Court proceedings are sometimes initiated by the Poor Relief authorities, if the wife had appealed to them for assistance; the result is the same.

LXXI.

Only a small contingent of convicted men work at Brixton, and these are specially selected. They are employed on odd jobs under the Works Department or the prison officers. Repairs to walls and roads, and distribution of fuel are among their activities; no, activities is the wrong word to use, for I have never seen so little accomplished by so many in a day's work.

The aim appears to be to fill in the time, whilst the results are immaterial—a bad principle.

The coaling party always seemed to find plenty of leisure to form an interested audience at our cricket matches, and made us a set of stumps on one occasion.

Tobacco was the currency in Brixton, not only amongst ourselves, who were privileged in this direction, but also amongst the debtors and convicted men, who craved this forbidden luxury; it was a pleasure to assist our comrades in misfortune.

Ethically our conduct was wrong, but the point of view changes considerably in prison, and nobody has a right to sit in judgment, who has not done a spell 'inside.'

Anyway we were only too ready to supply a long-felt want, when it could be done circumspectly.

For some months, I contributed in this way to the comfort of the coaling party who brought our fuel, and we all enjoyed the little game of hide-and-seek involved in effecting the transfer of contraband.

LXXII.

One man, a cat-burglar by profession, was full of good stories about his work: one concerning a visit to Lady Oxford was particularly fruity.

He wrote me a letter of thanks on behalf of himself and his comrades; here it is:—

Dear Sir,

On behalf of the four jolly sailors—sorry I mean jokers, we all appreciate your thoughtful present to us and rite to convey our thanks. Please don't think I am peaching of your generosity if at any time you feel similar disposed towards us re cigs or tobacco just drop them on the gravel when we are looking. Handing goods to us is likely to get you into trouble, will always be thankful whatever you do for us. Speaking for myself I can very likely return kindness in the near future as I am being released shortly.

>Good Luck and Thank you,
>One of the Jokers,
>or stokers.

P.S. Will do my best to make the lads a cricket bat at first opportunity as I see they like to knock the ball about and were using a strip of wood.
>Cheerio Sir,
>Better Days.

Destroy this note.
Put down lavatory and flush.

I did not obey his instructions, as I kept his *billet doux*.

When he returned home, he did me the honour of coming a long way to pay me an unprofessional visit. He knew the neighbourhood, about which my delicacy forbade too deep inquiry.

I should like to have assisted him financially, but I could not run the risk of promoting visits elsewhere of a more professional nature, in view of my own criminal record. However, we enjoyed a nice chat.

My family never forget to remind me of one old 'shipmate,' whom I did assist when he spun me a very plausible yarn, mentioning many of our mutual 'shipmates' by both name and nickname.

Subsequently the Superintendent of Police at Putney regarded me in a pitying manner, when I unerringly identified the visitor in the local Rogues' Gallery. I knew that he was thinking "Another bloody old fool, who ought to know better." I only hope that he has not added my photograph to his collection.

Upon one of my visits to Brixton to see a less fortunate companion still behind bars I was greeted vociferously by a number of convicted men employed in repairing the coping on top of the prison wall and I could not help realising that this welcome was open to misinterpretation by the passers-by. fortunately Jebb Avenue is a *cul-de-sac,* as I have already mentioned, and anyone who witnessed the incident was more likely to be a Samaritan visiting a prisoner, rather than a Levite: so I was comforted.

LXXIII.

We had ' C ' Wing to ourselves, except for a short time, when thirty Chinese seamen who had been serving sentences for refusing to go afloat, were added to our numbers, whilst awaiting repatriation.

A question in the House led to their removal. I had no objection to them, as they were inoffensive and cleanly. Fancy thirty Herbert Morrisons, for example!

LXXIV.

We christened an exercise promenade, in the shadow of the prison wall, close to our ground, the 'Death Walk,' because nearly all its frequenters went to the gallows. They were all persons ordered to be kept in isolation for some reason or another; mostly spies.

I can still see many of them in my mind's eye, padding up and down their solitary beat like caged tigers. Sometimes we managed to pass cigarettes to them.

An enemy spy in time of war is a brave man, and deserves to be shot, and not hanged, which is rightly regarded as being more ignominious.

LXXV.

In June, 1941, my family and I suffered a great sorrow in the loss of my elder son, missing, and believed killed, in Crete.

Everyone was most sympathetic, and I was especially touched by a letter of condolence from the Governor and the whole of the prison staff.

I asked the Governor to be good enough to try and arrange a special visit to Holloway gaol to see my poor wife, deprived of her firstborn in such cruel circumstances.

The Governor kindly did as I asked, but the clerk at the Home Office suggested that it should be made instead of my next fortnightly visit, when the car would be going in any case with Sir Oswald Mosley and retinue. He did not press the matter, when the Governor expostulated, but these are the little things one remembers, when the larger issues are forgotten. Even at such a sad moment for me, the little snipe could not resist a vindictive dig.

LXXVI.

My wife was released in November, 1941: it was a great joy to me, when she could come and see me.

These visits took place in a little group of visiting boxes, with a prison officer in the centre as listener-in.

Originally they had lasted officially for a quarter of an hour, but by the time my wife got out, the time had been extended to half an hour.

She applied to the Home Office for permission to come and see me twice a week, as she did my business affairs and correspondence, and was acting as wife-cum-secretary.

She was told that as the visits had just been increased to half an hour, that should prove sufficient for everything.

I wonder how they knew this. Fortunately I had arranged with the Governor for two visits a week, an arrangement which he was fully entitled to make, within his own discretion, so we said nothing more to the Home Office; but I thought quite a lot.

LXXVII.

About this time, Morrison, from his privileged position in the House, made a grossly misleading statement about the reasons for which persons in my category were detained, with special reference to myself.

Fortunately for me, one of the Sunday papers was foolish enough to rely upon this Minister's utterance, to publish a serious libel.

My solicitor, the late Mr. Oswald Hickson, handled the matter with great celerity. An apology appeared in the paper the following Sunday, and an apology in open Court, with a mention of agreed damages, on the Thursday following that. I attended to hear this apology, only regretting that it was the paper, and not Herbert, which was on the mat.

I never knew the Law could be persuaded to operate so quickly: I think it must have needed a master hand in the law of libel, to procure such galvanic action.

LXXVIII.

All through the winter of 1941-42, I had to watch impotently all my gloomy forecasts about the loss of our possessions in the Far East coming true, whilst the politicians were running round in circles, and talking the most abject rot.

The Japanese attack on Pearl Harbour was treacherous, masterly, and true to form. The Americans have only themselves to blame for their carelessness. They must have forgotten Port Arthur.

However it is no pleasure to say "I told you so," over such an ignominious business.

We have not been told all the truth about the Pearl Harbour affair up to the present; Roosevelt could have told us a lot more.

The dilemma in which the two buddies, Churchill and Roosevelt, found themselves, was the one I had foreseen.

In order to make Europe safe for Democracy, the United States must be brought into the war, to help defeat Germany.

The European war was distasteful to the majority of Americans, who smelt a rat somewhere. On the other hand, against Japan, a united front could be mustered; so Japan must be made to fight.

It has been admitted by Mr. Cordell Hull that the United States Government presented impossible terms to Japan, and only expected a declaration of war in response: it was here that they failed to profit by the lessons of history.

I do not pretend to know whether Churchill realised the speedy loss of our Far Eastern possessions which was bound to follow, if his efforts to bring America into the war were successful.

I can only reiterate that I did.

Let us hope that the loss will only be temporary: even so, was the price we had to pay for interfering in Europe, worth it?

Was it sound policy to set alight the British Empire House, in order to have the satisfaction of roasting the German pig?

Was the little bill in blood and treasure justified?

These are the sort of questions which all sensible people will insist on getting answered, if we are to have any better hopes of wiser Government in the future.

LXXIX.

In December, 1942, I decided to write a letter to Sir Irving Albery, M.P., who had taken such interest in 18B: fortunately letters to Members of Parliament could not be stopped by the authorities, or mine would have been on this occasion.

I intended originally to send copies to all Members, as I wanted to be sure they would have no excuse in the future for pleading ignorance of what they had done to their countrymen.

Eventually I only sent copies to a few of them, as I was assured that in most cases, both time and paper would have been wasted, as they were completely callous to the issue.

I addressed a bowdlerised edition to the Editor of the "Times," which I never expected to reach him, nor was I disappointed, but this letter formed the basis of a debate in the House, from which the victims extracted great benefit.

No Government sure of its position in the country, and confident in the rectitude of its policy, would have had recourse to such an iniquitous system as 18B.

The law of the land, even in war-time, is sufficient safeguard against any activities contrary to the interests of the State.

Offenders can be prosecuted with the utmost rigour of the law: the country would applaud, and the Government would be strengthened by its firm action.

Arbitrary arrest, without charge preferred, is a war essential, but a Government that finds it necessary to introduce an arbitrary form of imprisonment of indefinite duration, without charge or trial, thereby weakens its own position. It shews that there is something wrong with its case, which it is afraid of coming to public knowledge, and possibly slackening the war effort.

That is the most charitable interpretation that can be put upon this form of tyranny: once introduced, the way is open to every form of personal malice and vindictiveness, which have been given free scope on the present occasion.

The people whom the Government desires to put away by this means, are obviously those who have been too inquisitive about what has been going on, acting, in all probability, from the most patriotic motives.

If it were possible to charge any of these people with a misdemeanour, it is evident that the very things the Government desires to conceal, would be brought out in evidence at an open trial: even from a trial *in camera,* undesirable limited publicity would result. Hence 18B, prompted by powerful influences behind the scenes, and promulgated by the members of a British Government.

LXXX.

The text of the letter was as follows:—

> Brixton Prison.
> *December* 14, 1942.

Sir,

After two and a half years in Brixton Prison under Defence Regulation 18B, I have a few remarks to address to every Member of Parliament who cares to read them.

Not on my own behalf. I have nothing to ask from the men and women largely responsible for writing this very dirty page in the history of England. I want to make quite certain, however, that you understand fully what you have done in passing this legislation without adequate safeguards.

It is of little avail to prate of freedom and to practise simultaneously the worst form of tyranny in our history—the imprisonment of fellow countrymen and women without charge, trial or means of redress.

It is clear that many Members were misled by the Crown Lawyers who drafted the Regulation into believing that their provisions sufficiently protected the victims. In practice we are completely at the mercy of one man—the Home Secretary.

Until recently we thought that at least the conditions of our imprisonment were protected by Command Paper 6162. Now a High Court Judge has ruled that this Command Paper is so much waste paper as far as legal rights are concerned.

I cannot help feeling that some of you would be ashamed if you were aware of the 'reasonable causes' which are considered justifiable for the indefinite imprisonment of hundreds of people. The public were led to believe that we were persons who might help our enemies. That was "the most unkindest cut of all;" an unjust aspersion on many honourable men. But it was the only way to satisfy public opinion and at the same time conceal the real intention. The people have a touching faith that their Government would not shut up anyone without good reason. How little they know!

The veil of secrecy so carefully drawn over the proceedings of the Advisory Committee effectually prevents any knowledge of the strange uses to which the Regulation has been put from becoming public property. Many Members appear only to question those cases in which the Home Secretary exercises his right of differing from the Committee's findings. That is quite insufficient, unless the instructions to the Committee regarding the nature of 'reasonable causes' are also available. I doubt very much these ever having been committed to paper.

All the cases which have reached the Courts have borne out the dubious nature of the evidence used and the methods employed. In many cases both the Committee and the victims are kept in ignorance of the allegations upon which the Home Secretary reaches his decision. This he has specifically admitted. The usual reasons for this procedure are advanced: the protection of informers; secrecy in the public interest in war time, which can be used to cover a multitude of transgressions; and so on.

Are you aware:

1. That particulars received by the prisoner before confronting the Advisory Committee are vague statements which have little bearing on the case and are therefore of scant use to the prisoner?

2. That in addition, these particulars commonly relate to matters stretching as far back as before the last war?

3. That, in the course of the search on arrest, the prisoner is deprived of evidence bearing on his case and is refused access to it before his Committee hearing?

4. That the Home Secretary consistently refuses to state a case against the prisoner, thus making it impossible for him to defend himself?

5. That the assistance of a Lawyer during the hearing by the Advisory Committee is refused on grounds of security, whilst in high treason trials involving secret matters lawyers are admitted to Court?

6. That the prisoner is refused a copy of the shorthand record of his hearing before the Advisory Committee, without which it is impossible for him to check the accuracy of the record, or recall the wide range of matters raised?

7. That Members of Parliament making enquiries at the Home Office are sometimes given in confidence information about a prisoner which they cannot disclose to him and which he cannot therefore refute?

8. That any good lawyer could draft a procedure for the Advisory Committee which would safeguard the interests of the State as well as those of the prisoner?

9. That such a procedure would expose 18B as an ugly racket and prevent it being used any longer for ulterior motives?

The following colloquy, which took place at an Advisory Committee hearing between a prisoner (not myself) and the Chairman, illustrates some of the foregoing points:—

Prisoner: "May I be confronted by my accusers?"
Chairman: "No."
Prisoner: "May I have my lawyer at my side to assist me?"
Chairman: "No."
Prisoner: "Will you call witnesses for interrogation in my presence?"
Chairman: "No."
Prisoner: "May I question your witnesses?"
Chairman: "No."
Prisoner: "May I know who your witnesses are?"
Chairman: "No."
Prisoner: "Will you produce your evidence for my inspection?"
Chairman: "No."
Prisoner: "May I have access to my own material now in your possession?"
Chairman: "No."
Prisoner: "May I have a copy of the stenographic notes of this secret hearing?"
Chairman: "No."
Prisoner: "Will your findings be made known to me?"
Chairman: "No."
Prisoner: "Have I the right to appeal?"
Chairman: "No."

At this point the Chairman interrupted abruptly, saying: "I would like to remind you that you are here to *answer* not to *ask* questions."

The remedy is simple and is in your own hands. Naturally, trial or release is the only satisfactory method of treatment—the British method.

Failing this, the following conditions should be observed: they are not much to ask:

(a) That each prisoner may be accompanied by a Member of Parliament and by his legal adviser (or friend) when appearing before the Advisory Committee.

(b) That the particulars given to him should specify the real causes that have led to his integrity being called in question.

(c) That the Home Secretary should be bound to inform each prisoner, in the event of an order for further detention, of the precise reasons for the order, so that no doubt can possibly remain in the latter's mind.

I have used the word prisoner throughout this letter instead of detainee, as the High Court Judge to whom reference has already been made, ruled that this term was to be employed in his Court as it more closely represented our condition.

I hope sincerely the House of Commons will see their way to make this belated contribution to the cause of Justice and thus remove the blot which exists at present on our national reputation for giving a man a fair deal.

Every day that passes adds to your individual responsibility in this matter. I know that it is difficult for Members to arrive at the truth on account of the smoke-screen of innuendo and taboo which invariably envelopes the over-curious, but this is only the unfortunate corollary of the Regulation which the House saw fit to pass.

I do beg you to give this matter your most earnest consideration.

Yours Truly,

BARRY DOMVILE.

SIR IRVING ALBERY, M.P.,
House of Commons, S.W.1.

LXXXI.

Amongst other Members to whom I sent a copy of this letter in March, 1943, was Mr. John McGovern, and it fell on fruitful soil. Unbeknown to me, he must have taken the matter up with Morrison, and was, I have no doubt, largely instrumental in opening the gates of Brixton Prison for me on 29th July, 1943. He sent me the following letter he had received from Morrison:—

Dear McGovern,

You will recall that we had some correspondence about the case of Admiral Sir Barry Domvile, from which it would appear you were not happy as to his detention, and I think you would like to know that, following a review of the case, I came to the conclusion that I should no longer be justified in maintaining his detention. Instructions for his release have accordingly been given.

Yours Sincerely,
HERBERT MORRISON.

J. MCGOVERN, ESQ., M.P.

I do not suppose that I shall ever know why our little Pharaoh suffered this change of heart; he had no more reason to let me out, than to put me in. Possibly he came to the conclusion that my further detention might prove a liability rather than an asset.

McGovern is a persistent man, to whom several 18B's are indebted for their release. In any case, my warmest thanks are due to him, as well as to Admiral Beamish and the other Members of Parliament who raised their voices against this shocking business.

Several people have asked me, since my re-appearance in public, whether I had not expected my brother officers to attempt a rescue. Frankly, no. One of them would have, but he was dead. David Beatty was the only naval officer I have ever known, who was a match for the politicians, whom he treated with scant respect. He was rather Napoleonic in this direction, which was why some of them disliked him so much.

I have already related how he pinned down Winston on one occasion; no mean feat with that agile gentleman.

In my case, he would have gone to Churchill and Morrison, and told them that their action was very bad for the Service, and demanded that I should be turned over to my brother officers, who would deal with me far more drastically, if they found I had done, or contemplated anything, against the country's interests.

He would not have taken NO easily for an answer and generally he would have been a thorn in the side of Judmas and Co.

A lifetime of discipline and respect for authority gives most naval officers a pathetic faith in the rectitude of Government, which, I need hardly say, I cannot share.

EPILOGUE

I.

I spent three years and three weeks in the Royal Box, behind the grille, watching the puppet show, and now I am back in the pit again.

During the whole time I was in the Box, I kept my opera glasses focussed on the stage during the performance, and studied the programme carefully during the intervals between the acts. As a result, I came to certain definite conclusions.

I am no politician, by which I mean that I have never belonged to any political party, but I dare say I understand politics as well as the average man.

In the future, it is essential that as many people as possible should take an active interest in political affairs. In the past, too many people have been content to leave politics to the professional politicians; perhaps they did not realise how intimately everybody is affected by the proper conduct of national affairs, including their foreign aspect; perhaps people were too lazy and too trustful to study these things.

On the Continent, where foreign neighbours are unpleasantly close, a very different state of affairs exists; many people are surprisingly well-informed on foreign questions. Our welcome sea-barrier makes us less inclined to worry our heads about things over which we have no direct control, and which are not brought too close in front of our noses, until it is too late to do anything.

Largely as a result of being left too much to their own devices, our rulers nearly landed us on the rocks: that they failed to do so, lies mainly to the credit of the country as a whole, whose courage and determination were well to the fore, and not to the conduct of politicians who have progressively misgoverned us during the last quarter of a century, with the deplorable results we are witnessing today.

In future, we must keep a more watchful eye on these gentlemen, and not give them so much rope. I do not imagine for one moment that the electors who sent their representatives to Westminster in 1935 thought, if they thought at all, that they were giving the Government a mandate to go to war over Poland: on the contrary, no dove of peace could have cooed more softly for their favour than the average party hack on the hustings.

Nor were our politicians empowered to offer the French a common citizenship, or to pawn the West Indies to the United States, or in any other way to mortgage our sovereignty under the pretext of war duress.

It was the same old story. Once the votes were secured, the electors ceased to count, or the parliamentary puppets either, for that matter.

To put it plainly, our political machinery is in need of a thorough overhaul. Politics are dirty today, and will get dirtier still, if the Old Gang are allowed to carry on, as they are preparing to do, directly the "Cease F i r e " sounds.

I can already hear them shouting "Trust the men who won the war," and not, mark you, "Trust the men who made the war, and who are quite capable of making another, if they are not watched a bit more closely."

II.

The Party system, as it exists today, is largely responsible for the marionette show. When a man signs on at Westminster, he guarantees to vote faithfully for the Party otherwise he does not get the Party ticket, or the benefit of the highly developed Party machine.

Duly elected, he takes his seat in the Mother of Parliaments: when the whips crack, he trots docilely into the appropriate pen—perhaps lobby is politer—and chews the cud of irresponsibility: it is all done for him.

Gone is the sturdy independence which kept Parliament alive in the past, the dim past; now the puppets dance, whilst hidden forces pull the strings behind the scenes.

The trustful voters send their candidate to Parliament on the programme contained in his election address. That sounds all right, but he has no earthly chance of seeing his programme carried out, unless Party procedure happens to coincide with his election promises. It never does, in spite of the fact that these promises were written for him in the Central Office. Election promises are mere vote-catching bait, made to be broken; the party managers have bigger fish to fry. So the new member can only shake his head sadly, adjust his leading-strings, and behave like a good yes-man. The independent spirits are few and far between.

I should like to see Parliament full of stout-hearted young Independents, firmly determined to advocate the views of their constituents, and to vote according to their commonsense and consciences, and not as per three-line whip.

The old hands will say that this would only produce chaos—*quot homines, tot sententiae*—I do not think it would, but even if it did, better chaos created by honest men, than the present system of implicit obedience to the Managers of the puppet show—off stage.

More honesty and open-dealing are required in the conduct of foreign affairs, which today are shrouded in mystery.

The experts say that this is impossible, and that nothing would ever be accomplished, if secrecy in negotiation were abandoned in favour of more open methods. The experts must be overridden. We have all been led up the garden path in the past, and will be again, if we do not do something about it. It is very much our business, and more especially of the younger ones, who will be called upon to fight the next war, and not the men who make it, under the present system.

The present war was brought about by Hitler's challenge to Judmas; he was the first man since Napoleon, with the courage to tackle it openly.

His new economic and financial plans for Europe struck at the very roots of Judmas policy. It made war certain, if it could be arranged; it was arranged. There is no need to look further for a cause.

Churchill has told us himself that we entered the war voluntarily; that no British interest was threatened. Dear little Poland was the excuse this time; it was dear little Belgium upon the last occasion.

All the old battle-cries were trotted out; freedom, liberty (18B was the exception that proves the rule) and, of course, religion.

III.

The Archbishops, those two champions of Erastianism, with whom the Gold Standard and the God Standard appear to be synonymous terms, took the field.

Some people were a little uneasy about Russia, so the late Dr. Temple said in May, 1942: "I cannot see anything incompatible between economic Communism and Christianity. It was only a historical accident that Communism had been associated in any way with Atheism." I should like to hear Stalin's honest opinion on that amiable pronouncement.

After the discovery of the bodies of all the Polish officers bumped off by the Bolsheviks, a "refresher" became desirable. So the Archbishop of York, Dr. Garbett, flew over to Russia, but was only able to report on his return that the Bolsheviks were doing "so-so" on religion.

And what is the truth? I surmise that there has been more real religious feeling both in Russia and Germany in recent years, than exists in this country today.

Both Russia and Germany have tasted the bitterness of adversity, which breeds either faith or despair.

Prosperity, on the other hand, breeds religious humbug, hypocrisy and materialism; and we have been so prosperous; we could well afford to keep all our unemployed out of the churchyard and on the dole.

We must start our new career with a little more reality, and a little less humbug, in our search for the Good Life, which must include the greatest amount of personal freedom possible.

The most important Freedom of all—because the greater includes the lesser—is the Freedom from control by Judmas. This was not even mentioned by our two knock-about tragedians—the Churchvelts—in their Atlantic Chatter, or Sermon on the Mont de Piété.

Before I register my vote at the next election, I shall want to learn from the candidate that he is ready to pledge himself to tackle the Judmas problem, or, if he finds himself unequal to the task, to promise to resign in favour of a better man. Otherwise I don't vote.

Judmas is a canker eating out the heart of England, and every young man and woman in the country ought to take a hand in seeing that a satisfactory solution of the problem is reached, because they will reap the harvest that they sow. By the time the next war is due, I do not expect to be here, but I should like to see a good start made on a clean, new, England, before I depart.

IV.

When the liberal nations of the world have succeeded in dumping a sufficiently liberal supply of bombs on the "have not" nations, to make the latter realise that they "have not" got enough left to live in or on, and that they "have not" got any further desire to upset the tranquillity of the world, presumably we shall have peace.

What we make of that peace is important to all of us, but more especially to the rising generation, who can reasonably expect to see the results of their handiwork.

There are a great many people besides Israel and Rebecca planning the future of this country on widely differing lines.

All are agreed that the task is one of immense difficulty: their only common meeting-ground.

To those who will have the task of shaping the brand-new life of the country, I wish the best of luck.

I hope that they will have constantly in mind the supreme factor in the creation of a happy England, in a prosperous world; peace.

Peace—a long spell of peace, to enable us to develop our great Empire, which we have so grievously neglected, whilst we have been busily engaged in putting our finger into other people's pies, and contributing to the present disturbed state of the world.

V.

No peace can be expected to last for ever. Human nature will have to improve out of all knowledge, before that is possible. Progress, even in the right direction, must create divergent policies: discords result, which cannot always be settled without an explosion. Peaceful conditions themselves, carry the seeds of future strife. People become too comfortable and easy-going, defences are neglected and fall into disuse; the population declines in numbers; thus nations wax and wane, and envy and greed do the rest.

All the more does it behove us to try and eradicate any known factors likely to cause international dispute, so as to prolong as far as possible the period during which peace may be expected to last.

VI.

Amongst the most mischievous of these factors in the world today are the activities of Judmas, with their vast designs for the construction of a world Super-State, as the final goal.

Perhaps in theory the production of a stamp of international citizen is attractive to some people: in practice the difficulties are great. Every healthy nation wishes at heart to base its existence on its own characteristics and habits.

Such a desire is eminently natural, and it is no use trying to submerge it with woolly international theories.

We are proud, with good reason, of the British tradition of life, and have no desire to see it suffocated by the imposition of alien customs. This old country is too small to try experiments with a heterogeneous population, importing exotic habits and ideas, except to the small extent which has been the custom in past years.

On the other side of the Atlantic, the United States of America are engaged in a great experiment, trying to create a real American nationalism from the mixture of human material reaching their shores from all parts of the world, but even their Government got alarmed at the troubles they were laying in store for themselves by the establishment of too mixed a collection of races, and passed laws to reduce the ingress of foreign elements, excluding entirely the so-called yellow races, already arrived in large numbers, and limiting the nationals of other lands.

Recently, under pressure of war conditions, the ban has been lifted for Chinese. Notwithstanding all these precautions, the United States have a wealth of trouble ahead of them, before they can securely weld their human material into a real hundred percent American pattern. You will have all seen the varied types from across the herring pond, and have had an opportunity of judging for yourselves the breed which a mixture of races is producing.

There is no room for that sort of thing here. In spite of our falling birth-rate the country is still over-populated, and will be to an increasing extent, after this disastrous war, owing to the loss of markets abroad, and the increase of industrialisation in the rest of the world, to which the war has given an impetus. We have our own safety-valve for a surplus population, in emigration to the other parts of the Empire, so woefully neglected in the past, as a means of strengthening the British ties and heritage.

An outlay equivalent to one day's cost of this war would have afforded a welcome stimulus in this direction: we do not deserve to have such a rich slice of this world's living space, if we do not put it to a proper use.

Once the healthy life of this country is made possible by an attractive scheme of emigration to draw off the surplus population, the birth-rate will show an immediate improvement; lack of prospect is holding it back, not lack of fertility.

VII.

In the meantime we do not want to clutter up our homeland with all sorts of exotic elements, a process now going on.

We have always prided ourselves in the past on granting asylum to any foreigners seeking shelter under our hospitable wing.

British nationality has been granted them after they have fulfilled the easy conditions qualifying for naturalisation.

This had led in course of time to a generous admixture of various stocks in our national blood, and has presented no specific difficulties, except in the case of the Jews, who are in a category by themselves, through having no land of their own to which they can return.

Furthermore, no race has preserved its exclusiveness and its distinctive characteristics more carefully than the Jews, and their universality in all parts of the globe has enabled them to establish an international power, which has been used frequently, and furtively, to the detriment of international relations.

A certain number of Jews can be assimilated by any country, without much harm, but when saturation point is reached, the peculiar Jewish characteristics, which they claim to be due to their persecution in the past, have led to undesirable developments in the land of their adoption.

Unfortunately these alien symptoms have been especially noticeable in our own land for some time past, although only in recent years has attention been drawn to their menace to our national life.

In the interests of our own breed, it is desirable that steps should be taken as soon as possible to check the harmful symptoms already in existence, so as to avoid any increase in their influence in the future.

VIII.

With the foregoing in view, I invite the consideration of our people, and especially of our young people, to the following proposals, which will be discussed briefly under

the appropriate headings:—
 (1) Establishment of a Jewish homeland.
 (2) Review of the laws of naturalisation, and regulations regarding change of surname.
 (3) Abolition of Secret Societies.
 (4) Freedom of the Press.

IX.

(1) A JEWISH HOMELAND.

The Jews have never had a land of their own; the majority have no desire for one. Many have made themselves completely at home in the lands of their adoption, where their talents have often been employed to great advantage.

The important point to remember is that until a homeland to which they can retire is made available, it is difficult to introduce restrictive legislation in regard to their claim to naturalisation and asylum.

Once in possession of a land of their own, there would be less excuse for Jews to demand a home in other countries, and every encouragement could be given them to withdraw to their own.

Every nation would then be free to make its own rules and regulations with respect to Jews refusing to take the opportunity of emigration to their national home, in the same manner now employed for other individuals of foreign origin. There would be no question of unfair discrimination.

Opposition to this proposal will come from the Jews who are quite happy to remain where they are, as well as from the international contingent, who prefer dispersal for their race, in order to provide a nucleus of world power in each country.

Only the Zionists want a Homeland, and they only want one particular Homeland—Palestine, the Over-Promised Land.

The situation of a country for the Jews has been frequently discussed in the past.

Unfortunately for the Zionists, Palestine is out of the question, as it already belongs to the Arabs, who are naturally unwilling to be dispossessed.

On historical grounds, there is small justification for the Jewish claim to Palestine, as anyone who takes the trouble to study the subject can discover for himself. The Balfour Declaration was most mischievous, encouraging false hopes and thereby creating a real grievance.

The geographical situation of Palestine in the hub of the Great Continent, renders it unsuitable for the permanent home of a race, rightly or wrongly suspected of international mischief-making.

Furthermore, I have harboured the possibly unworthy suspicion, that Zionist anxiety for Palestine was engendered more by the natural wealth of the land, and especially of the mineral potential of the Dead Sea deposits, than by any genuine nostalgia for the country.

As long ago as 1903, the British Government offered a portion of the uninhabited territories of the East African highlands, through the good offices of Mr. Joseph Chamberlain.

Differences arose amongst the members of the Zionist organisation, and prevented the acceptance of this offer, which would have provided a satisfactory solution to a difficult problem.

At a later date, Israel Zangwill, the Jewish writer led an influential section of Jewry who were in favour of the scheme, but nothing came of it: the moment had passed.

It is interesting to note that Joe Chamberlain had been hard at work, at about the same time, trying to effect an Anglo-German Alliance, which failed mainly on account of the Kaiser's insistence on his naval projects.

In promoting these two widely differing, but all-important policies, Joe showed a far greater degree of foresight than was ever evinced by his offspring, Neville and Austen, or any other of our politicians of recent years, who have been content to follow the orthodox lines laid down by Judmas, although not necessarily conscious of this obscure influence.

It is heart-breaking to think of what might-have-been, and only a waste of time withal. Rather let us turn Joe's "might-have-been's" into our own positive achievements: only thus could we ensure a long peace, and have something to be more proud of than of a world laid waste.

Madagascar has also been suggested as a suitable locality for a Jewish Home, but there would be many objections here, and the Malagasy are already well established.

On the whole, the most promising proposal for a land of sufficient size to accommodate the fifteen million Jews in the world, and permit of further expansion, is Biro-Bidjan in East Siberia: Soviet Russia has already established an autonomous Jewish Colony of some considerable size there.

Lord Marley has visited this Colony, and says that accommodation is unlimited, and that no question of an existing population arises.

However this is a matter beyond my province. I can only emphasize once again the imperative need for a land to be allotted somewhere, so that the Jews can become once more a nation, established in a land not too alien to their own historical origin.

X.

(2) NATURALISATION AND CHANGE OF SURNAME.

Great changes are desirable in this direction: it is much too easy to become "English" today, by employing one of the processes mentioned in the heading.

Until this metamorphosis is effected, difficulties confront aliens who are engaged in endeavouring to penetrate our national life, and influence its course.

Our main object should be to prevent undesirable elements purchasing or controlling our organs of publicity.

These today consist of the Press, the Cinema and the Radio. As these media have a strong influence in shaping public opinion, the people who control their output obviously possess enormous powers for good and evil, which can be employed to affect the national traditions, morals and habits. Harmful influences have been at work to an increasing extent through these agencies in recent years.

The policy of newspapers can be controlled to a great extent, without the need for ownership, by means of the advertisements, which form such a large proportion of the income of a successful paper, that it cannot continue to show a profit without them; on the contrary, it would be run at a heavy loss.

This puts a tremendous power in the hands of big advertisers, who can, and do, threaten to withdraw their custom, unless any features in the paper, objectionable to them, are altered to suit their wishes.

In extreme cases, advertising patrons can boycott a paper out of existence: once the circulation falls it is natural for the advertisements to follow suit, and the decline is accelerated. Many will remember the case of the *Morning Post* and the "Protocols of Zion": members of the Bathurst family could tell a tale about this.

Unless the various organs of the Press are conducted by people with patriotic, healthy minds, unafraid of intimidation in any form, and conscious of their great responsibility, there is bound to be deterioration in the national outlook, such as has occurred in recent years.

There is ample reason to suspect a sinister design in the decay of principle and morality shown by a certain type of newspaper today; all this accords with the policy outlined in the Protocols.

The whole matter needs a thorough investigation now that we are embarking on a new era; we want to start our new voyage in a well-found ship, steadied on a true course.

Of course there are many other ways in which it is possible for camouflaged aliens to affect adversely our national life: membership of Parliament or of the professions enables alien sentiments and policies to be diffused throughout the various strata of society: these tendencies have also been very prominent in recent times.

Precautions are needed to prevent people from obtaining the full rights of British citizenship, unless they are prepared to co-operate whole-heartedly in the British tradition; even so, it may be advisable to restrict membership of certain spheres of action, to those of real native origin.

XI.

Change of surname is another aspect of the same question.

There is no law to prevent a man from taking any name he happens to fancy, nor are any unpleasant formalities involved.

It is not a crime to employ an alias, but if a man changes his name for good and all, it is customary to regularise this action by applying for a Royal Licence and publishing the fact in the Press, after execution of what is termed a Deed Poll.

People may desire to change their names for many reasons: they may possess an ugly name, or one subject to vulgar interpretation: they may be compelled to effect a change, if they desire to inherit money or property, the transfer of which is subject to that condition: they may wish to conceal their connection with some owner of their name, who has rendered himself notorious.

The most common reason of all, however, is business interest. This device is employed by aliens, and especially by Jews, who find that they can trade better if they are called Jones or Gordon, rather than Rosenbaum or Mosenstein. In reality these people are practising a deception on the public. We have the authority of Shakespeare for saying "What's in a name? That which we call a rose by any other name would smell as sweet." I beg leave to doubt that assertion, in the present connection.

The following extract from the *Fermanagh Herald* of September 1943 illustrates my contention:—

> "A resolution from Longford County Council, received and approved by Cavan County Council, urged that the Government's attention should be immediately drawn to the fact that a large number of foreigners, mainly Jews, have succeeded in changing their names recently by deed poll to names of Irish origin. The Chairman referred to a recent prosecution for fraud of a Mr. I. O'Hara, formerly Cohen."

When you come down to bedrock there are few really good reasons why people should be allowed to adopt a new surname at will, and the whole procedure needs tightening up. If everybody were forced to revert to their original surnames, we should find some surprising results amongst our acquaintances.

XII.

Here is another example within my own experience:—

When I went to H.M.S. *Britannia* in 1892, there was a Jew in the term above me called Albert Siegmund Susmann, I remember little about him, except that he had plenty of brains, and an ungovernable temper. I lost sight of him, and have no idea when he left the Navy.

Nearly half a century later, I addressed a newly formed Branch of the "Link." Shortly afterwards, I read a letter in a local paper abusing me and the "Link," and any thoughts of friendly relations with Germany. The letter was signed by a correspondent with the English name, A. S. Elwell-Sutton, the initials being the same as those of my brother cadet.

Perhaps I have a naturally suspicious mind: anyhow, I instituted enquiries, and discovered that here was my old comrade of the briny, writing under a thoroughly English name and running true to form.

Only recently I read in the same local paper that this gentleman had accepted an honorary post in a British Association for International Understanding, which had been formed for the purpose of "providing objective and factual information about all countries and peoples to its members, and the best means of countering tendentious propaganda."

Whilst not suggesting any improper motive or insincerity on the part of this gentleman, I feel certain that I shall go elsewhere for my facts and international understanding.

This is a very good example of Jewish activity in this country, in its efforts to influence public opinion. Had Susmann done it, it might have been suspect, but it came all right from Elwell-Sutton.

XIII.

These matters of naturalisation and change of surname, together with the subject of Secret Societies, which we shall be discussing presently, should be reviewed by some such body as a Royal Commission, empowered to take evidence on oath, and to recommend a definite policy in regard to all these things.

Meetings should be held in public, because we are all entitled to know what is being done about such an important affair, affecting our whole future. There will be a great deal of ground to cover, but the business should be dispatched as quickly as possible, and interim reports issued, because it brooks of no delay. The investigation is overdue. Much time and labour would be saved if the Jews and Freemasons concerned endeavoured to justify their conduct to the nation at large, instead of denying it, and thus requiring a lot of evidence which might have been dispensed with. Presumably many of them must have thought that they were acting *pro bono publico,* when they assisted to engineer this world cataclysm.

An anti-Jewish wave is sweeping across the world, and there is no smoke without fire.

Feeling has been rising rapidly in this country, and unless a thorough ventilation is given to the whole question, there will only be an outbreak of regrettable incidents which will disgrace our vaunted civilisation already beginning to look a bit moth-eaten as a result of this war, and the universal barbarity with which it has been conducted, which would have made the most abandoned savage feel queasy. And yet people took me to task before this war when I cast aspersion on the silly little rules which Eden and Co. were drawing up at Geneva, to make war a nice kindly pastime. I told them that there was only one Law that counted in war-time—the Law of Expediency: was I right?

XIV.

To return to our subject, the great thing is to get something done about Judmas.

The present situation has been reached largely through a number of well-meaning and liberally-minded people pooh-poohing the very existence of a Jewish problem.

Of course, there is a Jewish problem, and the sooner it is sensibly tackled, the better for all-concerned, Jews included.

One might suppose that the Jews would welcome an enquiry of the nature I have suggested: if they have nothing to conceal, and are prepared to justify their actions, nothing but good could result for them. The only people who would look foolish, would be the stupid ones like myself, who had made much ado about nothing.

But I am ready to wager a Lord Mayor's Banquet to a ham sandwich that the Jews will do nothing of the kind. They are already clamouring for legislation to be introduced to make "anti-Jewish" activities in any form illegal. They well know the wealth of irrefutable evidence available for exposing their machinations.

The usual tactics will be pursued over my mild proposals: this little tale of woe will be boycotted, neglected by reviewers, kept discreetly in the background at the library, if found there at all, and only "on order" at the stationer or bookshop. There is a well-organised conspiracy of silence on all matters critical of Jewry.

We are not concerned here with the petty offences, Black Market, and so forth, which can be dealt with by the ordinary processes of the law. It is the "tall poppies" amongst the Jews, whose dubious methods require investigation. Indeed the latter appear to welcome the attacks on their co-religionists, which appear occasionally in the Press, in regard to the petty offences attributed to them, and supposed to be of a specially Jewish character. These attacks arouse sympathy, and divert attention from the more serious charges which can be levelled against the "big-shots" of Jewry, who play behind the scenes with the policies of nations, as you or I do with the chessmen or the draughts.

I repeat again that nothing would be more distressing than to see an attack launched in this country on the Jews in general, as has happened in Europe, with such shocking results, entailing misery and hardship on perfectly innocent individuals.

Do not let us start the new voyage by disgracing ourselves. Let us rather try to focus the searchlight on those modest giants of Jewry, who so much prefer to keep out of the beam.

These men are committing no indictable offence by pursuing the policies of International Jewry, and attempting to get a stranglehold on the world through its finances, the Branch in which they specialise.

The people who are justly entitled to our blame, are those Englishmen, born and bred, who have allowed themselves to be made the tools of International Jewry, either for their own personal advantage, or in pursuit of some policy, which cannot be considered in the national interest.

Some of the latter may be sincere in promoting the schemes of Judmas: I hope so for their sakes.

Until a thorough investigation is made into all these activities conducted behind a veil of secrecy, there will be a lot of dissatisfied people in this land of ours.

These feelings will grow apace, unless some honest attempt is made to put things right, and to ensure that national affairs are conducted in the best interests of the people as a whole, and not in those of a limited and privileged section.

As good a groundwork as any other for the suggested public enquiry would be a thorough examination of the causes leading up to the war, and more especially the guarantee to Poland. No secrets need be left undisclosed, now that our civilisation must be rebuilt, and we are all entitled to know the why and the wherefore of the catastrophe. This examination would reveal undoubtedly many undesirable features in the pre-war handling of diplomatic affairs, and the necessary precautions against a recurrence would be indicated. We shall have earned the right to insist on all these matters being made public, by virtue of the ordeal we have undergone.

XV.

(3) ABOLITION OF SECRET SOCIETIES.

I approach this matter with diffidence; I have no desire to be impertinent.

Secret Societies have been the bane of many European countries in the past, and we do not want history to repeat itself here.

If the aims and activities of any society or organisation are innocuous, what need can there be for secrecy? Secrecy naturally leads people to believe that there must be some shady or sinister motive, requiring to be kept concealed from the public view. The British Encyclopaedia is vague and reticent on the subject.

In principle, nobody wishes to interfere with the freedom of others to form themselves into any fantastic sort of organisation they may desire, in pursuit of magical, religious or social objects, but in practice, during times of national unrest, such societies are undesirable on the grounds that they may be applied to subversive purposes.

This happened with the Klu Klux Klan in the United States, where Congress had to intervene. A later Klu Klux Klan, formed as recently as 1915, was indicted as a menace to decent Government by the Attorney General, and was proved to have been used for political bribery and corruption.

In this country, Freemasonry is far the biggest secret organisation, and claims a large and ever increasing membership. It has practically the monopoly of Local Government, and flourishes in most professions and trades.

I never became a Mason myself, for the simple reason that I do not think it right that anyone in Government employment should belong to any kind of secret society: you want to avoid the suspicion of benefiting by membership, in a manner unfair to non-members. The suspicion persists, however much Masons may protest that unfair advantage does not exist.

If we are to have that real equality of opportunity that we hear so much about today, in every walk of life, it is manifestly improper for some of the starters in the race to band themselves together into a secret organisation, which may, or may not, assist them in their chosen profession. I have seen enough of it in my own Service to make me very suspicious.

I have received many complaints from business men of the unfair advantages accruing from Masonry, and of the pressure brought to bear upon them to join, if they wished to prosper.

Many Masons have told me that the objects of the fraternity were purely benevolent: if that is so, why the secrecy?

XVI.

As far as political activities are concerned, the general belief in this country has always been that Continental Masonry was highly involved, but that British Masonry remained uncontaminated. That is untrue; Masonry in this country has been unable to resist the temptation of using its secret powers for political ends.

I am not in a position to judge to what extent it is involved in this direction with Continental Masonry, but I can make a pretty shrewd guess—up to the hilt.

Put yourself in the shoes of a Jew, engaged in promoting the aims of his international brethren, and anxious to acquire control of key positions in the Government of this country.

Whom would he be most likely to approach? Obviously those Gentiles themselves members of a secret organisation: and what organisation could he find more suitable than the one with which the Jews themselves are so intimately connected, and which they claim to have founded?

A certain amount of evidence of the complicity of English Masons in Judmas is available, much is merely circumstantial, but so circumstantial, that only a Judmas jury could fail to convict. As in the case of the Jews, the great majority of Masons are kept in ignorance of this side of their organisation's activities. Possibly the general resultant policy is handed out in the Lodges for compliance: I cannot tell, but it is difficult otherwise to account for the widely spread refusal to touch the Jewish question at all, which is mainly responsible for its hitherto unimpeded progress.

The grip that Jewry has upon our machinery of Government and organs of publicity, is positively uncanny: this can only result from the assistance given by Masons.

I cannot imagine anything more undesirable than an international organisation possessed of these secret powers for good or evil; it has got to be disbanded, if the world is to have any peace. There is no means of controlling the work of secret societies, short of disbanding them. This may sound unfair, but we cannot afford to take any risks. We are at the crossroads, and have to decide quickly whether we are content to continue with this alien grip on our national life, or whether we intend to be masters in our own house.

A great effort will be required to overcome the strength of Masonry in Government circles, and to obtain an enquiry into the whole affair.

There is nothing to prevent Freemasons from continuing their good works, provided they discard the paraphernalia of secrecy, but it is undesirable that persons in Government employment should be Freemasons in any case.

There are many other secret societies in the country, indulging in all sorts of queer practices and beliefs; signs of the times. None, however, has the scope or influence of Masonry. The objection to any secret society remains: secret societies and national reconstruction do not go well together.

I do not ask my readers to believe me implicitly, but I do implore them, in their own interests, and in those of the generations to come, to insist on a thorough enquiry into the working of Judmas by a Royal Commission.

If this is not done, their blood will be upon their own heads, and they will deserve anything that may come to them.

Now that national policy is in the melting-pot is the time for a thorough stock-taking.

To all those who love this land, and share my horror of the evils growing up in our midst, which can only end in the destruction of all we hold dear, I appeal with special confidence, to leave no stone unturned, to ensure that a complete investigation is made into the activities of the enemy within our gates.

We shall not be given another chance, and we shall not deserve one.

XVII.

(4) FREEDOM OF THE PRESS.

Anybody who harboured any doubts in regard to the advantages of a really free Press, must have been completely converted by the operation of Government censorship in this war which has put such a premium on the truth, that nobody is inclined to place much credence in what they read. This is bad, and brings the Press into more discredit than ever, through no fault of its own.

Notwithstanding the strictures I have passed upon the undesirable methods employed for controlling newspapers, a free Press when peace returns, is absolutely essential.

Newspapers should be free to print any news, and any comments, with one exception: any paper deliberately publishing falsehoods, with the ulterior motive of biasing public opinion, should be severely dealt with.

That the Editor knows an item of news to be untrue, does not prevent thousands of readers from believing it implicitly: that is where most of the harm is done.

In war-time, nobody expects the truth: any form of malicious propaganda is legitimate, more's the pity, but war is war.

It is, however, unpardonable for the Editor to publish in time of peace, items which he is not in a position to confirm, but which commonsense tells him are untrue, especially when, as is usually the case, they are items of foreign intelligence.

Private individuals have the law of libel to protect them.

It is quite a different matter to state a fact, and then ascribe to it a sinister and improbable motive; that is "fair comment." It may be deplorable, but, unfortunately, there are many deplorable people in Fleet Street.

XVIII.

I will give two examples of the deliberate lies to which I refer.

One day, not long before the war, I sat next a well-nourished elderly damsel at a luncheon party, who would not herself have hurt a fly. She opened the ball by saying that she supposed I had heard of the shocking treatment to which the "Czecho-Slovaks," released from concentration camps, had been subjected by the Nazis. I realised that I should have to buy it, so I professed ignorance. It appeared that they had all been inoculated with the germs of leprosy. When I pulled her leg about believing such nonsense, she got very cross, and said that she had read it in her morning paper, and it must be true.

On another occasion, I was visiting Dachau Concentration Camp. I looked at an English paper I had just received, which contained a harrowing story told by a Jewish refugee, who said that he had seen one of his comrades at Dachau soaked in petrol and burnt alive. In this case, the editor did append a footnote in small print, saying that he had no confirmation of this tale. Why rush into print with such an obvious lie?

One favourite trick is to splash some terrible atrocity story over front page columns, and to deny it in the next issue, as unobtrusively as possible, on a back page.

The Lie Factory should be reserved for wartime, and any products in time of peace should be published at the risk of severe penalties.

The names of the Board of Management of any paper, together with a complete list of shareholders, giving their real names, should be readily accessible to the public at all times.

XIX.

I have mentioned the principle essentials for the disinfection of the home, before starting to tidy it up, and make it snug and prosperous once more for British folk.

There are all sorts of political cooks preparing a savoury mess with this end in view. The young Conservatives have been busy, and have issued a pamphlet called "Forward, by the Right."

They have been going "Backward, by the Left" for such a long time, that they have got a lot of lost ground to recover.

Also they appear to have handicapped themselves unnecessarily by including some of the Old Gang.

I doubt if they will win the culinary prize: still, they have rediscovered the Empire, and that is something.

What a pity they lost it a few years ago. It was there all right waiting to be discovered, but they failed to see it through the mist of golden rain that was falling closer at hand.

I hope they have learned their lesson, and that it is not too late, and that our Empire, although punch-drunk, will be able to get on with its proper business of minding its own affairs.

Whatever happens, I hope that the political gangsters who have been running and ruining the country during recent years will not find themselves back in the saddle: men with the mentality of the pawnbroker.

I do not think Al Capone and his mates would be invited to revise the Federal Laws on the other side of the Atlantic. I feel sometimes that our gangsters would prefer to bring the Empire down in ruin, rather than leave something for wiser men to rebuild, and run on sensible lines.

Unfortunately, I have no hope that, like Samson, they would have the decency to include themselves in the destruction.

It is important to note that none of the menus concocted by the best known political chefs, contains any mention of financial reform, which many wise men regard as the *sine qua non* of a prosperous future. The latter want the Government to undertake the issue and control of its own money.

To an ignoramus like myself, this sounds to be an essential prerogative of any Government aspiring to be a free agent. Any such policy would deprive Judmas of its most powerful weapon, the producer of booms, slumps, and other delectable situations.

The desire to maintain the present system throughout the world is one of the root causes of the present war, to which attention has been called recently by the sham fight at Bretton Woods.

As our existing political parties are in thrall to the Money Power, no surprise need be experienced that financial reform does not figure amongst the entrées or sweets on any of the new food programmes.

XX.

I had almost forgotten one queer exhibit of recent years, Lord Vansittart, father of the cult known as Vansittartism, whose doctrine cherishes a hatred, amounting to mania, of anything and everything German. This man is unable to see a particle of good in eighty million fellow creatures. Shades of Victoria!

If there were many more like him in the Chancelleries of Europe, it is not surprising that there was a war.

All this hatred sounds lovely in wartime; just the stuff to give the troops! Get out the largest hypodermic and inject a strong dose of this virulent poison. Grand chap, this lusty abominator.

What a Black Record!

Regard him in the cold post-war light of disillusion, and he will not look so good. Remember his opportunities. For many critical years he occupied important positions at the Foreign Office: during the most vital of these years, he held the key position of Permanent Under Secretary, until he was moved on, or off, by Mr. Neville Chamberlain.

It must be difficult for a man in any walk of life holding views on any situation, which are clearly unbalanced, to allow impartial reports to reach the public.

Whether you trust Germany, or whether you harbour the gravest suspicions of everything that comes out of the Reich, you do not want to find your principal adviser on foreign affairs so heavily inoculated with Teutophobia.

Perhaps others know more about this man than I do.

Anyhow, in our new life let us find a hard-headed, large-hearted, broad-minded man, to give us the straight tips on foreign matters, and not a poetaster.

XXI.

Nearly a century has elapsed since Europe was shaken by a series of revolutionary explosions.

The year 1848 saw the end of the Chartist movement in this country; a revolutionary democratic agitation of considerable magnitude.

In this year Canon Kingsley, the well-known poet and novelist, issued a placard which is worth remembering to-day: there is a lot of truth in it:—

> "There will be no true freedom without virtue, no true science without religion, no true industry without the fear of God and love to your fellow-citizens.
>
> "Workers of England, be wise, and then you *must* be free, for you will be *fit* to be free."

ROBIN'S TREE,
   ROEHAMPTON VALE.
October, 1943.

www.ingramcontent.com/pod-product-compliance
Lightning Source LLC
LaVergne TN
LVHW030636080426
835510LV00023B/3389